Certified Sales Leadership Professional 'CSLP'

Body of Knowledge

Ontario | Canada

Books may be purchased in quantity and/or special sales by contacting the publisher at PO Box 57053, Unit 101, 5602 Tenth Line West, Mississauga L5M 0M5, Ontario, Canada, by emailing Hello@CCLMCanada.org.

Printed in Canada

First Edition, 2014

Second Edition, 2020

Canadian College For Leadership & Management 'CCLM'
PO Box 57053, Unit 101, 5602 Tenth Line West
Mississauga L5M 0M5
Ontario, Canada

Tel: +1 647 560 8760 | Toll Free (Canada/USA): 1 855 866 6355
Hello@CCLMCanada.org | www.CCLMCanada.org

Notice

The Canadian College For Leadership & Management (CCLM) publications and bodies of knowledge are developed through collecting, analyzing, synthesizing, evaluating, developing and documenting data and information that are available from public and private domains and sources. Such data and information are considered by the public as generally accepted practices, knowledge and/or skills. CCLM does not independently test or verify the completeness, accuracy, precision or validity of the data and information. The CCLM also does not verify or confirm the soundness or applicability of such data and information in any domain, industry or practice neither it confirms its compliance with any laws, regulations or standards. CCLM disclaims any and all liability for any personal injury, property or any other damages of any nature whatsoever, directly, or indirectly as a result of using any of the CCLM publications and/or bodies of knowledge.

The data and information and CCLM publications and bodies of knowledge are provided to you on an "as is," "as available" basis without warranty of any kind whether express, statutory or implied, including but not limited to any implied warranties of merchantability, fitness for a particular purpose, quiet enjoyment, systems integration, accuracy, and non-infringement, all of which CCLM expressly disclaims. CCLM does not endorse and makes no warranty as to the accuracy, completeness, currency, or reliability of the content, and CCLM will not be liable or otherwise responsible for any failure or delay in updating any content. CCLM makes no representations or warranties that use of the content will be uninterrupted or error-free. You are responsible for any results or other consequences of using the content of CCLM publications and bodies of knowledge, and for taking all necessary precautions using or applying such content.

Your use of the content is at your own risk. CCLM specifically disclaims any liability, whether based in contract, tort, negligence, strict liability or otherwise, for any direct, indirect, incidental, punitive, consequential, or special damages arising out of or in any way connected with access to, use of or reliance on the content (even if CCLM has been advised of the possibility of such damages) or that arise in connection with mistakes or omissions in, or delays in transmission of, information to or from the user, any failure of performance, error, omission, interruption, deletion, defect, delay in operation or transmission or delivery, whether caused in whole or in part by negligence, acts of god, failure, theft or destruction of, or unauthorized access to the content.

The information available on CCLM publications and bodies of knowledge is intended to be a general information resource regarding the matters covered, and is not tailored to your specific circumstance. You should not construe this as legal, accounting or other professional advice. You should evaluate all information, opinions and advice available on CCLM publications and bodies of knowledge in consultation with your professional specialist, or with your legal, tax, financial, managerial or other advisor, as appropriate.

Certified Sales Leadership Professional Body Of Knowledge 'CSLPBOK'

Table of Content

Table of Figures and Tables

CERTIFIED SALES LEADERSHIP PROFESSIONAL BODY OF KNOWLEDGE 'CSLPBOK'

Preface

Welcome to the Certified Sales Leadership Professional Body Of Knowledge 'CSLPBOK', by the **Canadian College For Leadership & Management 'CCLM'**. The body of knowledge comprises of the knowledge, skills and generally accepted practices that practitioners on the field of sales and business development are supposed to master. The **Canadian College For Leadership & Management 'CCLM'** has developed the **Certified Sales Leadership Professional 'CSLP'** Certification to be the leading certification for sales agents, business development officers, and account managers and everyone who practices sales and business development to help set a baseline for good practices, knowledge and skills for the domain and its practitioners, and support the personal development for practitioners in this field.

In this introduction, you will have the chance to learn about the **CSLP** certification, its body of knowledge, how to become certified, and certification renewal and further more.

What Is Certified Sales Leadership Professional "CSLP" Certification?

Certified Sales Leadership Professional "CSLP" is a certification for professionals who demonstrate knowledge, skills and competencies in sales and business development as per the requirements of the Canadian College for Leadership & Management "CCLM".

CSLP's are experts in leads generation and deals closure. They make excellent sales pitches, read their clients body signs smartly, develop great proposals and present them with a wow effect. **CSLP** becomes the de-facto for sales professionals around the world.

What Is The CSLP Certification Body Of Knowledge?

The **CSLP** BoK comprises of various themes of knowledge and skills which a **CSLP** must demonstrate competency in. A **CSLP**:

- Understands the basics of sales, makes calls, prepares excellent sales pitches and seals deals.
- Overcomes challenges in the sales cycle, influences clients and reaches agreements.
- Understands the basics of proposals, develops solid proposals using various tools and solid processes.
- Effectively communicates with peers, managers, subordinates and clients, using both verbal and none-verbal communication skills.
- Masters body language for self and others, learns how to translate facial, hands and other body signs to support leads capturing and sales deal closure.
- Presents solutions or products with confidence using various tools and delivers wow moments to help seal a deal.
- Negotiates for the best, and under stress with difficult clients and learns how to win sales deals.
- Is ethical, endorses and enforces ethical practices and respects people's rights in workplaces.

Should You Apply For CSLP Certification?

If you are a sales person, business development, or interested in sales and revenue generation, then, **CSLP** certification is for you. With **CSLP**, you earn the knowledge and get the status and recognition.

Various people are pursuing **CSLP** certification, including, but not limited to:

- Sales executives, associates, business development officers and managers.
- Marketing professionals, coordinators and associates.
- Supply chain, bid and procurement professionals.
- Managers, store managers, clerks and many more.

What Is CSLP Certification Exam?

The certification exam tests your understanding of the certification body of knowledge. For the **CSLP**, the exam:

- Has 50 multiple-choice questions.
- Must be finished in 1.5 hours (90 minutes).
- Pass mark is 60%.

What Are The CSLP Eligibility Requirements?

In its effort to promote sound and solid professional practices and skills in leadership, management, strategy, executive assistance, sales, marketing and human resources, and on the same time, expedite the process of earning the CCLM prestigious certifications, the Certification Board at the Canadian College for Leadership & Management CCLM has decided to make the certification available for all candidates as of August 1st, 2017. Therefore, candidates no longer need to submit an eligibility form before taking the exam.

How To Apply?

The application process is very simple.

- Register for a course in our Self-Paced Training Courses.
- Or Order the textbook from Amazon and study it.
- Register and pay the examination fee.
- Book the exam online and pass your test.

Are You Looking For Exam Preparation Courses?

Exams preparation courses are offered in traditional instructor-led classroom and online through Registered Partners or directly at CCLM. Visit our online course calendar at www.CCLMCanada.org to learn more.

Do You Have To Renew Your Certification Status?

Yes. Certified professionals have to maintain '**active**' status of their certifications by renewing it every three years. Each certification has a number of recertification hours that must be met.

As a **CSLP**, you have to demonstrate that you have **30 hours** of professional experience in sales in a three-year cycle.

How Do You Renew Your Certification?

- Submit an online Recertification Application at www.CCLMCanada.org.
- Pay the recertification fee.

Do You Need More Information?

Visit our online FAQ section where you will find answers to most commonly and frequently asked questions at www.CCLMCanada.org, or contact us directly at Hello@CCLMCanada.org.

THE CERTIFIED SALES LEADERSHIP PROFESSIONAL BODY OF KNOWLEDGE CSLPBOK.

The Certified Sales Leadership Professional Body Of Knowledge CSLPBOK comprises of eight chapters as follows:

- Chapter 1: Fundamentals of Effective Sales Skills
- Chapter 2: Handling Sales Objections
- Chapter 3: Effective Proposal Development
- Chapter 4: Effective Communication Strategies
- Chapter 5: Mastering Body Language
- Chapter 6: Effective Presentation Skills
- Chapter 7: Effective Negotiation Strategies
- Chapter 8: Business Ethics Essentials

Certified Sales Leadership Professional Body Of Knowledge 'CSLPBOK'

FUNDAMENTALS OF EFFECTIVE SALES SKILLS

- Sales & Marketing: Which One Is First!
- Speaking Sales!
- Find Your Leads!
- Start Selling!
- Define The Unique Selling Position!
- What To Do When A Customer Says No?
- Sealing The Deal
- Following Up
- Your Sales Goals

S elling is a true translation of believing in something; a product or service. Sales of products and services are the main fuel for businesses and organizations. Estée Lauder, the co-founder of Estée Lauder Companies, the cosmetics company, once said *"I have never worked a day in my life without selling. If I believe in something, I sell it, and I sell it hard."* Effective sales people believe in what they sell, whether a product or service. Once they establish that belief from within, they understand the product, they live it and entirely feel it, they will have the magic and power to convince people, and turn them from prospects to customers and clients. As they believe in a product or service, they identify what would interest a potential customer, and entice him or her to spend their money. Effective sales people just know how to do this perfectly.

In this Certified Sales Leadership Professional certification body of knowledge, you will learn how to sharpen your sales skills by following a specific sales process and deploy effective tools. You will learn how to plan for your deal, master talking, craft a strategy, deliver a sales pitch, create a proposal and consistently and passionately follow up to close the deal.

1.1 Sales & Marketing: Which One Is First!

Typically, sales work hands in hands with marketing. Marketing agents will deliver messages about company's products or services using different means and methods such as Internet, TV commercials, billboards… etc. These methods aim to build awareness on consumers end, and hopefully initiate a desire. At one point, a potential consumer would initiate a call or make a visit to your company's showroom; it is at that point, when your effective sales skills have to flourish.

Other people would argue that it is actually the sales agents who deliver the company marketing message and, for instance, walk door to door with products flyers, or initiate a telemarketing phone call, neverthe-less, in this body of knowledge, we consider that a legitimate, legal and ethical sales process is the one that starts after an awareness has been made about a company products or services as indicated in the high-ly-adopted marketing funnel concept; AIDA.

Market funnels are traditional tools used by marketers as they contain the stages that a customer takes on the way to purchase your product. The funnel may vary slightly, but there are basic stages in the **AIDA** fun-nel that remain the same. These stages are **awareness, interest, desire, and action**.

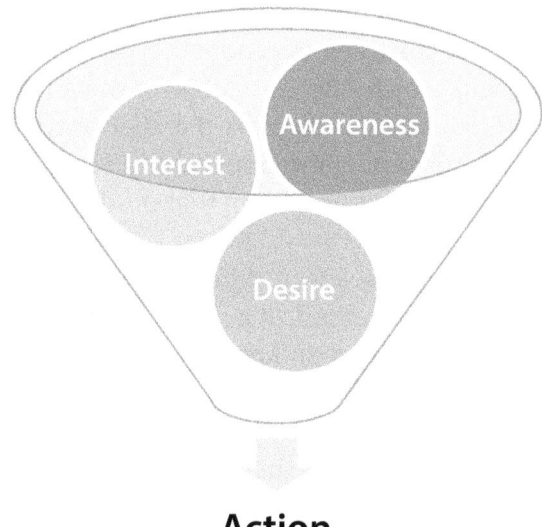

Action

Figure 1 – *AIDA Marketing Funnel*

The first stage of the marketing funnel is Awareness. This is the stage where the consumer is first exposed to your product through adver-tisements, word of mouth or billboards. Awareness can lead to the next stage of the funnel; Interest. Effective marketers ensure that awareness is always a positive experience. Then, comes the second stage of the marketing funnel, which is interest. This happens when the customer actively shows interest in your product. This is the point when a customer initiates the first action through a phone call to your company or a visit to a local store. We advocate that it is at this point when a sales process kicks off. Effective sales people convey their belief in a product through key persuasive messages that demonstrate the value of their products to the customer. They explain product features, benefits, compare and contrast with other competitors' products, and passionately elaborate why the customer would be satisfied or successful with the product or service. When you successfully engage interest, customers will be able to reach the desire stage.

Once a customer expresses desire to own the product, effective sales people would then offer product demos or samples. They work to intensify such explicit desire. They could offer flexible payment plans and work closely with the customer to ensure they take the last action; the action of purchasing, which is the last stage of the AIDA model. Sports stores like SportChek offers customers the chance to try their fitness equipment. Giving customers the opportunity to try products would encourage them, in many cases, to own that product.

When selling, sales people adopt different approaches; either relationship-focused or task-focused. In a relationship-focused approach, the sales professional focuses on knowing the customer first, understanding and analyzing their wants and needs, and offering a best-fit product or service. This approach is often lengthy and requires trust and confidence to exist between the seller and buyer. In products that require technical expertise or certain specialty; sales professionals tend to seek support from subject matter experts (SME's). While this approach of selling might not necessarily lead to an immediate purchase, however, it lays down the foundation for long-term relationship between the seller and buyer and increase the chances for repeated businesses.

On the case of task-oriented selling, the seller focuses on pushing a sale forward, especially for customers who have not yet reached the point of a 'desire' of your product. This hard sell technique might jeopardize the success of the whole selling process if customers feel they are threatened or uncomfortable. With this approach, sellers tend to use aggressive sales tactics such as imposing tight deadlines to purchase a product or offering aggressive price discounts. These temptations might work with some customers, but not with all. In today's corporate world, effective sales professional understand when to use each technique and in what scenario.

Sales Approaches (Relationship vs. Task-Focused Selling)	
Relationship-Focused	Task-Focused
• Works best with corporate or wholesale customers. • Focuses on more sustainable pricing and after-sales services. • Usually, sales orders or volumes are large in value (tens of thousands or millions of dollars). • Combines both direct and indirect selling through tendering, contracts and proposals. • Focuses on building a sustainable relationship, and repeated business, and not necessarily making a profit from the first sale.	• Works best with retail or one-time shoppers. • Focuses on one-time aggressive sales offerings. • Usually, sales orders or volumes are small in value. • Mainly focuses on direct selling and direct purchase orders. • Focuses on closing the deal on hand and make a profit from this deal.

Table 1 – *Relationship vs. Task-Focused Selling*

1.2 Speaking Sales!

In the world of sales, sales professionals use their own words and terminologies to express different things. As a seller, the most critical and important concept you might encounter is price and profit. Price is the value of the product or service, which combines the cost of producing it plus an acceptable profit for the company. It is the profit that companies care about most to fuel their operations, cover their overheads, and pay their shareholders.

Effective sellers develop a sales pipeline, which is the list of prospective opportunities or clients based on marketing information, sales leads, previous deals or contacts. A lead is any information about someone or an organization that shows an interest of your company product or service. Sales professionals maintain active database of their leads using software applications such as CRM or Customer Relationship Management applications. A call from a customer is a lead, a chat with your friend during which you learned that his boss is inquiring about a product your company sells is a lead. At this point, sales professionals collect lead information such as contact details of the person and what they are interested in and subsequently initiate contact to qualify the lead and the potential client.

Figure 2 *– A Sales Pipeline Process*

Qualifying a lead aims to understand whether your product or service satisfies the potential client wants and needs and whether the client's need worth considering. It often starts with a cold call because the client does not know you, and subsequently followed up with several warm calls. The qualifying process requires meeting or talking with the client, networking with them, analyzing and discussing your offerings and basically laying down a solution. Undoubtedly, client qualification process would also confirm whether the client is serious and would have access to funds and approvals to eventually make a purchase. Once assurances are established, a lead is converted to a deal.

A deal happens when the client is offered sufficient details about the product or service, its offerings, prices, benefits, and all information they need to make the final informed decision and take an action to place an order. This is when most of the effective sales tactics would take place. At this step, you have to clearly identify the person in the organization who could make a decision and owns the purchasing power. Once all requirements are met and the client is satisfied with the deal and proposal, they would place an order and make a purchase. This is the official closing of the deal.

For corporate deals, this process tends to be lengthy, especially if there is a contract or legal agreement that has to be put in place. Sales people are encouraged to have a minimum level of understanding of the contracting process in the organization, and must keep close eye on it till the actual final agreement is signed. Clients usually tend to issue a Letter Of Intent (LOI) to demonstrate their intent to purchase a product or service, however, an LOI does not constitute as a final and formal order and many clients tend to cancel them for various reasons. Effective sales professionals keep pushing and managing the contracting process till ltimate closure.

> *Effective sellers develop a sales pipeline, which is the list of prospective opportunities or clients based on marketing information, sales leads, previous deals or contacts.*

Once a contract or agreement is signed, and the sales order is confirmed and takes place, your role as sales professional does not necessarily finish. It actually has just started, especially if your selling approach is more of relationship-focused. You must ensure that products or services have been delivered successfully to the customer, and you keep checking on them frequently. This role is often referred to in organizations as Account Management; which is part of sales and customer relationship management. If your organization has this role clearly defined, you have to ensure you manage the transition of the client carefully to the new account manager. If it is you who manages the customer account after the sale, then, customer relationship management is of a paramount importance.

1.3 Find Your Leads!

As indicated earlier, identifying the lead is the first step in building your sales pipeline and selling. You might have been referred to someone, or a friend has emailed you the contact details of his manager. During networking events, there is huge opportunity to connect with people and identify potential clients. Your company online forum or contact form might also be another source for new leads. Whatever the source is, you have to gather as many leads as you can to build the first element of your sales pipeline. Once you have established your database of leads, you need to examine them to see whether they are decision makers in their organizations or not. You can use online resources such as social media, or public statements for publicly traded companies, or seek friends' advice. It is crucial not to waste your time chasing the wrong person; instead, you have to focus your energy and time on finding the decision makers or people who can influence a purchase decision.

Once a lead is identified, it is time to initiate a contact. Most likely this would happen over a phone call. Before you place that first and critical phone call, you have to be prepared. You need to capture as much information about the person you are calling, their actual needs and wants and be ready to respond to their various questions about you, the company and the products or services you are offering. Be ready to hear answers such as 'Well, I am not interested now' or 'Can I call you later as I am in a middle of a meeting'. Despite these frustrating answers and reluctances, you should not give up. You are just warming up.

As a salesperson, you will be making many cold calls to customers who never expect a call from you. The purpose must be clear, you have to gather as many information about their need and spark an excitement about your product or services. You have to entice them to learn more about the product or service offerings; nonetheless, this first call should not be lengthy or overwhelming. You need to do more of listening than talking and put the potential client on ease and relax to tell you their areas of pain, and why they should work with you to solve their business problems.

When you first speak to the lead, it will be influential to let them know who referred you to them. By letting them know that you have done business with a person they trust, you will immediately become trustworthy in their eyes, and would feel more relaxed to answer your questions and engage in a constructive discussion with you. In this discussion, you should expect all types of questions from your lead such as:
- Who you are, and what you do in your company.

- What the company main business is, its location, number of people, number of clients…etc.
- What your products or services are.
- How these products help my organization overcome certain business problems and challenges.
- How these products will be supported and maintained.
- Whether your company offers training and team development as part of the offering.
- Whether your company offers financing and flexible payment plans.

Practically, before you make the first cold call, you need to list down all possible questions that would come from the potential client, and draft brief answers to each and every one of them. By doing so, you get the best out of this first call and enhance the chances to develop the lead into a deal at later stages.

During the first call, you might be able to provide some suggestions to the client problems, if they look to be simple and straightforward, nevertheless, do not be tempted to jump to conclusions, you are still in the fact finding stage. During your research and analysis about the lead and their business problem, you have identified technical problems that you can not understand or help find preliminary solutions to, it would be advisable to ask some experts or SME's to join your first call, ever, ensure to make the first call short and productive, and use it to he stage for subsequent face-to-face meeting or further technical discussions.

> **As a salesperson, you will be making many cold calls to customers who never expect a call from you.**

1.4 Start Selling!

During the 'Lead' stage, you establish a rapport with the potential client; you make the first call and gather preliminary information. Now, it is the time to follow up with a meeting or face-to-face discussion to sell your product or service. In this first meeting, you have to look professional and provide an outstanding first impression. Be formal and profession-al in how you dress, walk, talk and present, and pay attention to your body language, verbal and non-verbal cues, voice, tone and gestures. In meeting new potential clients, there is no room for jokes or silly mis-takes. The potential client must have confidence that you are ready and equipped to help them overcome their business challenges and you are taking them seriously.

If you have been referred to the potential client, it makes a difference to start a conversation by sharing your experience on how you helped the referrer overcome their business problems. You can use this as an icebreaker and an entrance towards discussing the potential client own business challenges. You must appreciate that both business problems could be different, hence, do not prolong the discussion on the refer-rer problem, and instead move on smoothly to the potential client own problems.

To make the most out of this meeting, groundwork, solid analysis and research should be ready to support your discussion. Subject matter ex-perts should join you in this meeting should you expect the discussion to be too technical. By demonstrating to the potential customer that you have done your own homework, they would appreciate your efforts and product or service offerings. What your preparation tells them is that you understand their problems and come prepared with answers solutions, and not just trying to sell them something they probably not need or does not meet their criteria. At this point, they look at you as a true business partner.

> *The central point in any sale is getting the customer to see why what you are offering them is better than any competitor's offering.*

When analyzing a client business problem, conduct an online research for what their competitors are doing, read industry articles or special groups white papers, or seek SME's expertise. Your SME's might need to develop a prototype, mockup or a demo version of your company product to better demonstrate how your product will solve the client problems. Do not offer the one-size-fits-all solution. Clients are usually smart and they would pinpoint a solution that is made solely for them or just another demo product. If you initially consider the lead to be worth pursuing, hence, you should take extra steps to ensure that the prototype or demo product solves the client problem.

Once you have made it past the opening, it is time to make your sales pitch. In preparing your pitch, work on coming up with a clear, persuasive explanation of what your product can do for the client. Be prepared to answer the all-important question that all clients have: What is in it for me? This is, after all, the basic question in all financial dealings. If you are trying to persuade people to part with money they have earned, you may well need to work to give them reasons to do so. The central point in any sale is getting the customer to see why what you are offering them is better than any competitor's offering, and that you will see that their best interests are served.

When making a pitch, it is important to get the balance right between attractiveness and believability. You can promise the earth to a potential customer in order to get them to sign on the bottom line, but if they do not believe you can deliver on what you are offering, then it will be completely pointless. Also, as most deals have a "cooling off" period, the chances are that if you oversell your product, they will be dissatisfied and bring the deal to an end before it has had time to become established.

During selling, sometimes the relationship between a particular feature and its benefit seems obvious. For example, a self-setting clock on a DVR has the obvious benefit that you do not have to set the clock, but a salesperson might expand on this benefit by saying something like this: *"If the power goes out or you have to unplug the DVR, you do not have to read the manual to figure out how to reset the clock."* It is a good idea to describe benefits in explicit terms. This is not because customers do not have the intelligence to work it out for themselves, but rather because they will often be looking at a deal from a point of view of why they might be best served by keeping their money in their wallet.

In order to convince a customer to part with their money; it is essential to deal with any objections and to make them see how the benefits outweigh the cost. Therefore, a DVD player that you are selling may be a "multi-region" model. Simply saying that it is "multi-region" is telling them something they can work out for themselves by reading the box. The "multi-region" element of the DVD player is a "feature". The "benefit" in this situation is that they can buy DVDs from other countries and play them on the same system. In many cases, DVDs will be cheaper from a different country in a single-region format. Buying a "multi-region" DVD player will save them money, and so is beneficial to them. It is things like this that make a person purchase a specific item. The question that they may ask on the surface is "what does it do?" but the question you need to answer for them is "what will it do for me?" One item may have various selling points for different possible purchasers. It is important ✿ ɘ aware of what tack you should take with each customer. A sales pitch is absolutely not a "one size fits all" matter, for the salesperson or for the customer.

> *A sales pitch is absolutely not a "one size fits all" matter, for the salesperson or for the customer.*

1.5 Define The Unique Selling Position!

Some people assume that price is always the deciding factor in purchasing decisions. In fact, these decisions are often based on a variety of factors, such as:

- **Convenience of use**: One of the major attractions in buying any item is what kind of difference it makes to day-to-day life. People will spend money on any number of things to simplify their living situation.
- **Convenience of purchasing**: It may be that a high-value item is just out of a customer's reach in one payment. In such a case, being able to offer a payment arrangement will often make the difference between the customer signing on the dotted line

and them refusing to purchase. Flexibility in other areas is also beneficial.

- **Special features**: Any customer will be keen to get the best they can from a deal, and there are several "informed" customers who will be keen to make a set stipulation before agreeing to a purchase. Offering them a few extras on the item; which will increase the benefit to them, is a good way of encouraging them to sign.

- **Availability of service**: The customer does not just want to know that they have got a good deal; they also want to know that it will stay that way after they have taken the product home with them. Whether it is in terms of a competent help-desk telephone number or a dedicated technical department, this is something that will convince the less technically minded people.

- **Need for training to use the product**: More of an issue in terms of corporate sales, but not specifically limited to that field. The more "ready to go" a product or service is, the more immediate the benefit and the more likely the customer may be to purchase it. However, if training is necessary, this can still be a way in to make a sale, as the training can be bundled in with the purchase of the goods at a considerable discount as a way of convincing the customer.

- **Reliability of the product**: An in-store demonstration is as far as you can go to "prove" the reliability of a product. However, guarantees can be given in the shape of a warranty or another similar agreement, which covers the customer should the item not live up to their wishes.

- **Reputation of the seller**: The best demonstration of reputation is word of mouth, but most companies will have promotional literature, which can refer to easily checkable statistics or include testimonials from past customers. Knowing that customers tend to go away happy sets many people's minds at ease.

- **Friendliness of the salesperson**: It is a cliché, but nonetheless holds true the vast majority of the time. People are far more likely to make a deal with someone who makes them feel as though they are being taken care of. A salesperson who says "Hello" and introduces themselves, and then gives any information in an unfussy, respectful way is far more likely to get a sale than someone who asks "Can I help?" and gives all the appearance of hoping that the answer will be "no" before launching into a very cursory and jargon-filled sales pitch.

Of course price is important, it will frequently be a deciding factor in a purchase, but bear in mind that most people start out with a set budget in mind when looking to make a purchase. Therefore, as long as the item you are aiming to sell falls within that set budget, you ᶦld give as much time to other concerns such as those listed above. goal is not a simple, straightforward matter of persuading them to buy from you, but also a matter of persuading them not to buy from someone else.

A salesperson with expertise will turn reluctant customers into happy customers.

To make the point clearer, a customer's objections to buying some-thing are not the opposite of their reasons why they should buy it. It is therefore not the case that you can just reel off a list of reasons why someone should buy something and imagine that this cures their objections. In reality, it is more complicated than that and you need to highlight the positive aspects of the item while dealing with any negatives. You should also be ready to "sweeten the deal" with refer-ence to many of the above terms. If there is room to maneuver on payment terms, this may persuade the customer that they are getting a good deal. If you can give them a discount on peripheral equipment to increase the benefits of the item they are interested in, this may also work.

Customers are always asking, "What is in it for me?" This is another rea-son why it is important for salespeople to focus on benefits rather than features. Sometimes salespeople are so enthusiastic about the features of their products that they forget to explain what the products will do for their customers. Customers might not care about all the wonderful features of your products, but they will care about how your products will solve their problems or make their lives easier.

If we suspend disbelief for a moment, imagine that tomorrow someone invented a machine that woke you, got you out of bed, dressed, and fed you before taking you to work and doing your work for you. If it then took you home in the evening, made you dinner and did all of this while providing sparkling conversation before tucking you into bed at night, ready to repeat the cycle the following day and kept you fit and healthy into the bargain, it would be worth investing in, without a doubt. But would you buy it if all you knew about it was from a sales pitch which described it as having a "24/7 facilitation setting" and being "usable in a range of locations"?

The technical terms which are listed as specifications in the manufacturer's literature will certainly be enough to convince people who are technically minded and have been scouring the industry magazines for a period of time looking for the right model, but for many people there is only one question: "What is In It For Me?" That question should be answered in a few sentences at most, setting the customer's mind at ease and allowing them to put any follow-up questions that they may have. The likelihood is that they are not buying it for any of a whole list of reasons, but for one specific one. The fact that they show some [illegible]c ignorance of what else the product does means nothing in terms of their being prepared to pay the agreed price, so battering them over the head with "tech talk" is self-defeating.

You can overcome customer's objections if you are prepared to respond to them in a calm and rational way.

1.6 What To Do When A Customer Says No?

Customers who are not ready to decide on a purchase often come up with objections, statements about what is holding them back. You can overcome these objections if you are prepared to respond to them in a calm, rational way. Often, all that customers need is more information to make them feel more confident about their purchase. In these situations you need to be careful not to start an argument with a customer or belittle the customer's concerns. In fact, you might decide to agree with a customer to a certain point but then show the customer a different way of thinking about the purchase. For example: "I know that buying new windows is a big investment, but let's look at what you can expect to save in energy costs."

There is a saying: "If life gives you lemons, make lemonade". Although this is something of a cliché and not 100% applicable, it gives a good example of how you can deal with customer objections by turning them to your advantage. Naturally, people will be reluctant to part with money that they have worked hard to earn, and will not want to spend without being absolutely convinced that the spending has been worthwhile. This means that they will be on the lookout for things that will make the purchase less worthwhile. Your task, as a salesperson, is to hear and understand their objections but convince them to look at things differently.

Customer's objections may be challenged. If you listen to what they have to say and offer a different way of looking at things, they have the potential to be turned into positive reasons for purchasing. Often from minary conversations, it is possible to foresee what objection will and how to counteract that objection, and by your command of the situation you can convince the customer that you know what you are talking about.

> **Common customers' objections may include the following:**
> - *They do not have the money.*
> - *They can not get financing.*
> - *They can not decide on their own.*
> - *They think they can get a better deal from someone else.*
> - *They are not sure your product will meet their needs.*
> - *They think your product is overpriced.*
> - *They want to shop around.*
> - *They have an established relationship with another vendor.*

There is a sense in which sales are all about control. If you fail to produce a counter-argument for one or more of the customer's reasons for not purchasing, then you have conceded control to them and, more importantly, to their pessimism regarding the purchase. How you handle customer objections can be the major influence on your success in making a sale. Anyone can sell to a customer who is on a mission to make a purchase. Selling to someone who is determined only to buy when they are convinced of a good deal is a far bigger test. The customer might say that they can not afford your product, does not like it or worse is they have strong personal ties to another vendor.

In these situations, it is probably not worth responding to a customer's objections. Nothing you say will change the customer's mind. If they cannot afford the product, then they cannot afford it. Short of you giving them the money, you can not influence that and if you can not extend the payment terms then there is nothing more to say. If they do not like the product, you can offer alternatives but these may not have much relevance. If their objection is related to having strong personal ties to another vendor, then they may well already have made their mind up, but it is worth considering an approach based on the idea that a change is often a good idea. These responses are however at best speculative.

If the objections are less "firm", then they do have the potential to be turned to your advantage. If the objection is based on cost, then look at creative ways around that. It may be that they do not want to spend so much in one go. A payment plan may be the quickest way around this. A certain amount each month might be something they are prepared to do. You can also look at how much money the deal might save them over time. Saying "Yes, $300 sounds like a lot, but when you consider how much use you will get from the product and how much it will save you, it works out quite reasonably" can help. Avoid using words such as "cheap", as it can be insulting to a customer who is spending a lot of money.

If the customer is reluctant to purchase because they feel that the product does not meet their needs, get their needs ironed out and explain how the product does just that. It may be a good idea to call on your experience and mention that another customer had the same objections, but the purchase worked out for them in the end and now they ar by it. You can always embellish on a story if you can base that embellishment in something which holds up to analysis. The key point is to emphasize that the product has many more benefits than negative aspects, and to chip away at the negative aspects by presenting ways around them.

How do you respond to the following objections?

That's more than I wanted to spend.	How much were you thinking of spending? Do you know about the trade-off between price and reliability?
I'm not ready to make a decision.	What additional information would be helpful to you?
I'm not sure this product is right for us.	What features are you looking for?
I'd like to shop around some more.	What other brands are you considering?
I'm too busy to make a decision right now.	When can we get together when you have more time?

In dealing with customer objections, you want to come across more as a consultant than a salesperson. Even though the customer is a customer and you are a salesperson, if they feel like they are being "sold to" rather than dealt with like a human being, they will be far more likely to walk away from the sale. You need to keep away from appearing as though you have dollar signs in your eyes. This is where it is essential to maintain a balance between being a salesman and acting as a friend. Some salespeople make the mistake of trying to be too "friendly" and chatting to every customer as though they were talking over drinks. While this may work for some customers, it will backfire in most situations.

You are in the position of a specialist. If you were about to go in for surgery, you would not want the consultant to look down the list of symptoms and "jokingly" quip "Do you know any good undertakers?" While sales and surgery are clearly different, it is worth bearing in mind that the customer is not parting with money lightly. A salesperson with expertise will turn reluctant customers into happy customers.

1.7 Sealing The Deal

You have worked hard to get your foot in the door, tell customers what your product can do for them, and respond to any objections they might have. Now it is time to seal the deal, or is it not? A good salesperson needs to know when it is time to close and how to go about doing it.

Misidentifying the moment to close can carry numerous problems with it, not least the fact that a customer with extra thinking time can very easily suddenly decide that they are not so interested after all, and a customer who is pressed to complete the deal too early can be left with a negative impression of the salesperson, one which may be impossible to conquer.

The point at which it is advisable to close on a deal will be fairly obvious to any experienced salesperson. The moment will become apparent, usually after you have gone through a typical sales pitch, responded to the potential customer's objections and talked them around, and they have begun to give a positive impression with regards to buying, whether they do this verbally or through their body language and non-verbal comportment. At this point, you should begin to speak as though they are going to buy, while not talking as though they have already bought the product or service.

Once you start picking up signals that it may be time to close, you can ask a "confirmation question" such as "How soon do you need this?" If the customer gives you a date, you can proceed with the closing. If the customer still has objections or questions, you will have to handle those first. This process of asking a confirmation question is sometimes called a "trial close." The benefit of a confirmation question is that it is something of a "closed question". That is to say that it does not allow for the possibility that someone will come back and say "actually, I do not think I want it". If the customer is minded to buy the product, then they will already have been eased along the path to purchasing it by a simple question. Rather than asking "So, would you like me to package this up for you?" the confirmation question allows you to garner that information without having to put the customer in a position where they answer a "Yes/No" question.

At this point, it is more than likely that the customer's verbal and non-verbal signals will already have given a big lead as to their intentions. If they are making statements which pertain to where in their house the product would fit, or how they would use the service, then they are clearly already picturing themselves with the item, and they are as likely as they ever will be to be receptive to an attempt at closing. The nature of your closing technique is important here, but the main thing to remember is that as long as you are respectful to any concerns they may have, you are all but guaranteed the sale.

A closing question should give customers alternatives other than yes or no. This approach effectively closes the deal but makes the customer feel that they are in charge. You might wish to ask the customer on delivery dates, colors, models or quantities they wish to order. Craft a question that does not have a "yes" or "no" answer, allowing the customer to feel that they are in the driving seat while edging them towards deciding what you want them to decide. For instance, you may wish to ask: "So, when were you thinking of having the item installed?" "We do have a range of colors in which you can have the item, which of these do you like best?" "Well, there is this model, and there is another here with some extra facilities, which of those would you prefer?" or "How many of these items would you like?" All these questions give the customer the feeling they are leading the discussion and bring you closer to seal the deal.

It can be tempting to add at this point that other customers have tended to go for this color, or that many items, or to suggest when they could have the item delivered. It is wise, however, to avoid doing this as it looks like little more than over-efficiency and pushy salesmanship. Rather than doing this, you should pause and allow the customer to

✿ : the next word. If they are not a hundred per cent decided on the item and have a follow-up question, they may resent you talking in a way, which more or less celebrates the fact that they have decided to spend their money. What they say next will be the springboard for what you want to say, whether it be to formally close the sale or edge them further towards buying. Remember, they have not bought anything yet, and they are not "other customers".

> *A closing question should give customers alternatives other than yes or no. This approach effectively closes the deal but makes the customer feel that they are in charge. You might wish to ask the customer on delivery dates, colors, models or quantities they wish to order.*

Most people have had a buying experience that they felt good about. They were happy with the product and the terms of the deal. They may have felt so good about the experience that they told their friends about it and patronized the business again. Often this kind of good feeling is a result of being treated with warmth and respect by salespeople, before, during, and after the closing. Remember that the impression you make in the closing is the one that will stay with the customer. Try to make the experience as positive as possible. The way that you treat a customer will have a real impact.

This can be very straightforward and simple, and just requires you to be polite and friendly. You should always ask what more you can do for the customer, whether it be something like getting them an earlier delivery ✿ expected, helping them out to their car with the item or just asking n how you can help further. It may seem like some of the above tips are self-evident, but it is surprising how often customers come away from a buying experience feeling like, although they have completed the transaction as they came to do, they would not be in a hurry to buy from the same place.

> *The closing is not the final stage of a sale. The final stage is following up, which is actually a process that may continue indefinitely.*

All the same, you should not grin like a Stepford Wife when making a sale as this can be off-putting. Just being polite and friendly when closing the sale, and wishing the customer a good day as they leave the store can make a huge difference. What you can do practically, and how you do things, will serve you well in any sale.

1.8 Following Up

The closing is not the final stage of a sale. The final stage is following up, which is actually a process that may continue indefinitely. This stage may have two valuable outcomes: referrals and future sales. The nature of a follow-up to a sale will depend on how the sale was carried out. If you sell via mail, then the delivery should be accompanied with a compliments slip thanking the customer for their order and making clear your hope that you can do more business in the future. If you sell in person, then it can be very beneficial to follow up with a call a few days later asking how they have found the item.

When you carry out the follow-up, it is important to leave the customer feeling like they have been well treated. It is likely that you can think of a case where you have been given excellent customer service, you probably told your friends and family about it, and when you have required anything in the same niche you will have thought immediately of the salespeople that covered your sale and gave you such excellent service before. You will want to ensure that you receive that level of service again. As a salesperson, this is how you want people to think of you, too. By providing an excellent level of service every time, you will gain more business from the friends and family of that customer, and from the customers themselves.

Thank you notes are signs that you are interested in building a long-term relationship with a client. They show clients that you value their business and that your interest in them did not end when you closed the sale. We hear very often in this day and age of a lack of politeness and many people decry the cursory way that transactions are carried out. Although almost all companies make a great play of offering "excellent customer service", there is a world of difference between saying that you offer something and offering it every time.

The effect of a "thank-you note" is to make a customer feel that they have been more than just a number. They will read a thank you note and feel positive about their purchase. It has been proven time and again that we as humans have what people call "sense memory", where we associate a certain feeling with a certain occasion, incident, or place. If, for example, a certain song was playing at a certain time in our lives, we will always associate that song with that occasion and how we felt at the time. By the same token, a well-written thank-you note with a personal

A good example of a thank-you note would be along the lines of:

"Dear Emily,

Thank you for considering us when you decided to purchase a Healthy Life 2012x machine and for choosing us as your vendor.

I hope it gives you hours of pleasure and makes your activity easier. If there is any way we can help you in the future, with this purchase or another, please do not hesitate to contact me at +1 800-900-8888 or email me at Greg@healthylife2012x.com

Thank you again, and kindest regards,
Greg"

touch will stand out in a customer's memory. How you write the note is up to you. Obviously you do not want to spend more time writing thank-you notes than selling, but taking the time out to write one that shows you remember the customer (as opposed to "Dear X, Thank you for buying Y, we hope it is working well for you. Regards, Z") may well be what it takes to encourage them to come back to you when they need something else, and pass your details on to anyone they know who is planning to buy in the same niche.

Pitching a note at the right level is important. It does not need to measure up to Shakespeare or Oscar Wilde, but at the same time it is important not to write something that sounds as warm and personal as a pre-printed card. A thank-you note can be personalized to a greater or lesser extent depending on your area of business.

Providing excellent customer service after a sale is essential to maintaining strong relationships with customers. Starting at the closing, tell customers that they should feel free to call you any time to discuss any problems or questions related to your products. If a customer has a problem with a product purchased from you, try to see the situation as an opportunity. If you can demonstrate to customers that you really are committed to helping with their problems, they will think more highly of you, your company, and your commitment to customer service.

This is another example of a way that you can turn a potentially negative situation into a positive one. "Customer Service" is a lot more than just a phrase. When a customer comes to you or calls you, it is important not to simply play lip service to their enquiries. Should a customer complain to you that a purchase they have made from you is not living up to their expectations; your first response should be to get to the heart of their complaint. Your response should be along the lines of "Oh, I'm sorry to hear. What is the problem?" From their response to this, you should be able to think of a few solutions to that.

There are three elements to be taken account of in your response to a customer problem: **efficiency, politeness, and thoroughness**. All customers with complaints will want their problem to be dealt with speedily. In doing this, you need to find the right balance between "too quick" and "too slow". Many people take an attitude to problem solving which seems to suggest that the last thing they want to be doing is dealing with problems as it holds them back from going to do what they consider to be their "real job". However, the way that you deal with problems has a real impact on customer retention. It is best to deal with them quickly, but to be fully aware of what the customer wants before going straight into a process of solving the problem.

The above point is linked to politeness, naturally you will want to solve any problem quickly, but if you do not pay attention to what the customer wants and needs, and take the time to apologize for any problems then they will feel like you resent them taking up your time. Without a reasonable, polite attitude from you, they may well simply wait for their problem to be solved and then take their leave of you. If you are polite and understanding, this will stick in their mind. It is essential to consider that the final impression given to a person is the one that will resonate most. If they have a problem with an item but you solved it, and did so quickly and politely, then it will be the latter fact that stays with them.

The final point is that you must be thorough with your problem solving. From the nature of a customer's problem you will either know how to solve it so that it does not reoccur, or know someone who will be able to do this. There is sometimes a tendency to go for a quick fix ("Have you tried turning it off and then on again?") This is far from advantageous, as the chances are that the problem will be back again before too long. This will not help the customer, and will not help you retain the customer. If you deal with the problem quickly, politely and completely they will be happy to come back again when they have another purchase to make, and their overall impression of your company will be "When I had a problem, they solved it".

After sale service is not the only way to stay in touch with your customers. Here are some occasions that might prompt you to get in touch with established customers, such as:
- The anniversary of a sale
- A workshop offered by your company that the customer might find worthwhile
- The customer's birthday
- A new product offering
- A sale or special offer
- An upgrade to the product you sold

These occasions can all be marked quite effectively on a computer-based calendar and reminders can be sent to you via e-mail. This will allow you to then contact the customer and ask them a few questions in regards to how the product is working for them and so forth. Showing that you remember them even after a year, or that you recognize the proximity of a special date for them, demonstrates a personal touch in how you deal with customers, a touch which will mean a lot to them.

The most effective way to stay in touch with a customer is to retain certain information on them which can then be sent through the post or e-mail to alert them of another potential purchase they could make. It is likely that your sales niche will contain a number of different sections itself. Once you know what they have bought before, you will understand more about where their needs are and be able to point them to a new purchase that you think will help them. The key is not to contact them with a straight sales pitch right away, unsolicited sales pitches are rarely welcome, but to alert them to something that they might be interested in. By doing this, you give them a chance to make a purchase without putting excessive pressure on them.

✪ ing in touch with a customer can have a range of benefits from the simple fact of keeping yourself in their mind if they should have another purchase to make, to putting the idea of another purchase into their head. It is a form of advertising, with the benefit that there is already a link between yourself and the customer. If you can keep a personal touch in the contact that you make with the customer this is all the better, as they will remember that you did and think of you as a person to do business with.

> *The three elements to be taken account of in your response to a customer problem are: efficiency, politeness, and thoroughness.*

1.9 Your Sales Goals

If you want to accomplish anything important in life, you need to have goals. Goals give you something to shoot for, they keep you focused and motivated and they let you know when to celebrate and when to start shooting for something higher. Setting sales goals is not any different. By setting and achieving your sales goal consistently, you can benefit in a number of ways, you will gain recognition, potentially advancement within the company, and frequently will benefit from financial incentives.

Sales goals provide direction. They help salespersons in organizations focus on selling their products or services and overall well-being of their organizations. Without sales goals, salespersons are more likely to waste time on random activities that are not worthwhile. Your sales goals should be ambitious but realistic. If you set your sales goals too low, they will not inspire you to do your best and most likely will be challenged by your superior, without mentioning the fact that they could be less financially rewarding to you. If you set them too high, you will probably not reach them, and you will end up just being discouraged.

Also, sales goals clarify your role and responsibilities. Each member of a team has individual goals that contribute to the team's overall goals. Setting individual goals avoids duplication of efforts and makes people feel personally responsible for their work. Your sales goals can be also a motivational tool. It is difficult for people to feel inspired about their work if they feel they are just doing the same thing day in and day out, with no end in sight. Goals give people the feeling that their work is contributing to something larger, something worthwhile.

The benefits of goals are clear; it is how you react to the presence of sales goals that will mark how well you do as a salesperson. The idea of having goals is that they should be something achievable while not being easy. If you can attain your goals while working on autopilot, then the motivational impact of having them in the first place is somewhat lost. At the same time, if the goals set for you are too extensive, there will be at best a limited chance of you achieving them, and the over-all effect will be a de-motivating one as nothing you do will be quite enough to see you attain them.

Figure 3 – *SMART Goals*

Goals also need to mean something. If your sole reward for attaining a goal is to simply know that you have achieved it, then it will have limited impact on your motivation. You probably already know that you could attain these goals, but if there is no material reward for so doing you may be left wondering why you actually bothered. For this reason, most companies will have an incentives package which pays out when you meet your goals, and this will focus the minds of even the more cynical salespeople. The benefit of targets for salespeople is that they make a belt-and-braces approach, motivating those for whom achievement is its own reward, and those who expect more tangible, material rewards.

In setting your sales goals, use the SMART matrix, and define SMART goals. SMART goals are:

- **Specific**. Goals should be well defined and clear to you and your coworkers.
- **Measurable**. Goals might include milestones that help you measure your progress and make sure you are on the right track. The goals themselves should also be measurable.
- **Achievable**. Goals should be based on a knowledgeable assess-ment of what is possible. Unattainable goals discourage rather than encourage.

- **Relevant**. Goals should reflect the basic values, mission and products of your organization, and they should be directly related to your vision of success.

- **Timed**. If you do not have a timetable for reaching goals, you will not feel a sense of urgency about them. It is natural for people to devote most of their effort on any given day to things that have due dates.

The best goals are simple, one-sentence statements that anyone can understand. When setting goals, fewer words are better. Setting too many goals can be counter-productive. Focus on goals that will have the greatest impact on achieving your vision of success. Some companies, knowing that goals are a significant motivational tool, really go overboard when setting them. They will give their staff targets on several different measurements, some of which will contradict the others. It is also fair to say that an important element of setting SMART goals is calibration. There is every chance that targets will be set for the first month that are either too easily achieved, or too difficult. By looking at how people have performed in relation to their targets, it is easy to see whether they have been set too high or too low, and the targets can then be adjusted. It may take a month or two to get targets to the right level, as it is important to avoid over-correction. Once this is done, you should have a set of achievable but challenging goals which will bring the best out of staff and provide a motivated working environment.

Chapter 1 – Fundamentals of Effective Sales Skills

Q1- Sandy has been a Sales Manager for 20 year in kitchen appliances, and recently switched jobs to sell motorbikes. Sandy has never owned or ridden a motorbike before and shows no interest at all. Her knowledge is extremely limited. After several months, she missed her sales target. The key reason behind Sandy's performance is:

- A- Motorbikes are hard to sell as few people rides them
- B- Sandy requires training into motorbikes features so she is better equipped to sell them
- C- Her sales targets were impractical, and she should have approached her manager to revisit such targets
- D- Sandy's interest is lacking, thus impacted her ability to convince people and sell.

Q2- AIDA, as a marketing funnel, starts with:

- A- Ability
- B- Awareness
- C- Plan
- D- Action

Q3- In _____ the sales professional focuses on knowing the customer first, under- standing and analyzing their wants and needs, and offering a best-fit product or service.

- A- Task-focused approach
- B- Relationship-focused approach
- C- Timeline-focused approach
- D- Product-focused approach

Q4- Trust and confidence between buyers and sellers are key in:

- A- Task-focused approach
- B- Relationship-focused approach
- C- Timeline-focused approach
- D- Product-focused approach

Q5- In _____ , the seller focuses on pushing a sale forward, especially for customers who have not yet reached the point of a 'desire' of your product.
- A- Task-focused approach
- B- Relationship-focused approach
- C- Timeline-focused approach
- D- Product-focused approach

Q6- For task-focused approach, the seller:
- A- Mainly focuses on direct selling and direct purchase orders.
- B- Focuses on more sustainable pricing and after-sales services.
- C- Works best with corporate or wholesale customers.
- D- Considers tendering such as RFPs.

Q7- A chat with your friend during which you learned that his boss is inquiring about a product your company sells is a_____
- A- Deal
- B- Account
- C- Lead
- D- Customer

Q8- _____ happens when the client is offered sufficient details about the product or service, its offerings, prices, benefits, and all information they need to make the final informed decision and take an action to place an order.
- A- Deal
- B- Account
- C- Lead
- D- Customer

Q9- Clients usually tend to issue a Letter to demonstrate their desire to purchase a product or service. This is called:
- A- Contract
- B- Deal
- C- LOI
- D- RFI

Q10- In selling, USP Stands for:
- A- Unified Selling Plan
- B- Unique Selling Position
- C- Unified Selling Position
- D- Unique Selling Plan

Answers

Q1- The correct answer is (D-Sandy's interest is lacking, thus impacted her ability to convince people and sell) as belief and interest is key in selling.

Q2- The correct answer is (B-Awareness)

Q3- The correct answer is (B-Relationship-focused approach)

Q4- The correct answer is (B-Relationship-focused approach)

Q5- The correct answer is (A-Task-focused approach)

Q6- The correct answer is (A-Mainly focuses on direct selling and direct purchase orders)

Q7- The correct answer is (C-Lead)

Q8- The correct answer is (A-Deal)

Q9- The correct answer is (C-LOI)

Q10- The correct answer is (B-Unique Selling Position)

HANDLING SALES CHALLENGES

- Most Common Sales Challenges
- Framing As Opportunities
- Touching The Right Nerve
- Meet In The Middle
- Give Them The Driving Wheel
- Maintain Communication
- Follow The Process
- Dos and Don'ts
- Be Ready To Close

Everyone who works in sales will run into different sales challenges. From retail employees on the sales floor to sales executives, people at every level of the business need to learn how to overcome sales challenges and turn them into opportunities. Professional salespersons realize that the act of selling requires persistence and patience. Asking customers to surrender their hard-earned money for a product or service they are not quite sure they need requires shrewdness, patience and perseverance from the salesperson side.

In this chapter, we will continue the discussion further on handling sales challenges and objections, professional salespersons will come to learn the main and common sales challenges, how to frame them as opportunities, find common grounds with their customers and reach agreements to eventually close a deal. It is needless to say that mastering such skill requires also patience and a lot of practice, so start today!

2.1 Most Common Sales Challenges

Customers typically introduce sales challenges and objections for three main reasons. They may be skeptical of the product or service. It is also possible for customers and sales associates to have misunderstandings and miscommunication. Occasionally, however, customers may just be stalling. Part of overcoming objections is identifying the factors behind them. First of all, people are naturally skeptical. It is important to gain the trust of prospects and communicate effectively in order to prevent skepticism from developing into an objection. There are several ways that conversations with prospects can breed skepticism such as:

- **Lack of rapport**: It is important to develop a rapport. This requires listening and showing genuine interest in the prospect.

- **Poor questions or answers**: When speaking with prospects, you need to ask questions that will uncover their needs. You also need to answer the potential customers' questions completely and thoroughly and avoid the temptation to minimize their questions.

- **Moving too fast**: Never rush a presentation; people tend to feel you are less than truthful when they feel rushed.
- **Overpromising**: People do not trust promises that seem too good to be true. It is essential that prospects understand how an organization will meet its promises.

The second sales challenge is misunderstanding. Every relationship experiences misunderstandings, and misunderstandings happen easily when you are meeting with prospects. Communication is essential if you want to prevent misunderstandings and engage the prospects. There are three steps that all sales people can take to help prevent miscommunications. First of all, you have to clearly identify the need. Be sure to understand exactly what your prospects need and how you can help. Then, you must understand their goals. Ask the prospects what their goals are and how you fit into their goals, and finally, provide specific benefits to your prospects, do not give generalizations about your product or service. Explain exactly how your company will meet the needs and goals of the prospects.

The three main reasons for customer concerns are: skepticism, misunderstanding and stalling.

The third common challenge is stalling. Occasionally, prospects turn to objections in order to avoid making a decision. There are different reasons why people stall when they are with sales representatives. It is important to understand why people stall in order to determine how you should proceed. Prospects may not be authorized to decide. If the prospect is not authorized to make the final decision, meet with the person who is. Your prospects may want to compare companies, in this case, try to make sure that you are the final interview. If your prospect is not convinced of your offerings, ask what questions you can answer to help. The final resort prospects tend to use is the excuse of lack of time or money. Counter this challenge by setting a definite time to meet that busy prospect and work out a specific budgetary figure or payment plan to meet their 'lack of money' excuse.

2.2 Framing As Opportunities

Sales representatives need to expect prospects to make objections. Rather than seeing objections as hindrances, they should be viewed and framed as opportunities. Addressing objections early on will help prevent any problems later on in the business relationship. Simply learn to translate the objections to questions and reasons to buy.

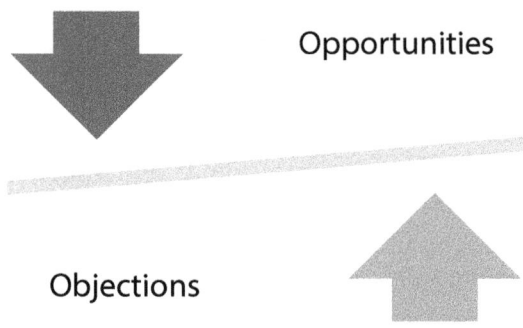

Figure 4 – *Objections As Opportunities*

Objections can indicate that a prospect is interested in what you have to say. Therefore, objections should be welcomed and encouraged. It is possible to translate objections into questions and explore ways to overcome them. Practicing this technique will provide the opportunity to understand exactly what the prospect objects to and alleviate any concerns by answering their questions.

How to frame an objection to an opportunity?

Prospect: I'm afraid I won't use the product in the coming weeks before its expiry?
Salesperson: So, you are saying that you are concerned that product will expire before you use it all?
Prospect: Yes, I am.
Salesperson: No need to worry, our product has an expiry date of 2 years, and if you think you will not be using it in the first year, you would still have a 90 day return policy, no questions asked! What about that?
Prospect: That's really nice.

Sometimes the objections that prospects give are actually good reasons for them to buy. It is the sales representative's job to point out how the objection is actually a benefit. A client may object to the change in the business your product would bring. The change, however, could lead to greater profits or open up a new clientele. This sales objection can be overcome by providing clear information and statistics that show the prospect the benefits of buying.

2.3 Touching The Right Nerve

When handling objections, you need to ask the right questions in order to develop a positive rapport; or touch the right nerve. Every salesperson should be prepared to face objections. Most customers have the same common objections. This means that you should have a number of appropriate questions ready to handle the different objections. We have already established that you need to translate objections into questions and then opportunities. It is important to remember, however, that asking the wrong questions or even asking the right question in the wrong way will not encourage your prospect to make a purchase. You need to remain professional at all times, and never take objections personally. When asking questions, there are a few things you need to remember to do and not to do such as:

- **Allow the customer to finish**: Always ask the question when the customer is done speaking.
- **Be positive**: Believe in your product and allow the customer to see that in your demeanor.
- **Maintain eye contact**: Keep appropriate body language to earn trust.
- **Be prepared**: Work testimonials and statistics into your questions.
- **Do not argue**: Being defensive or sarcastic will not win any new customers.
- **Never tell the customer that they are wrong**: Even when people are wrong, avoid pointing it out.
- **Do not accuse the customer of not understanding something**: Make sure that your questions are not insulting. Ask for clarification rather than insulting a prospect's intelligence.

After they listen to your sales pitch, people may give different objections such as your product is expensive. At this point, you have to ask them something similar to: "May I ask what you are comparing it to? Did you know that the quality of our product results in fewer purchases from our customers?" Other prospects might say that they are not interested to pursue a deal, you may respond by saying: "I understand that you are not interested at this time, but may I explain how we can increase your profit margin?" Or they say they need time to think about your product, you may respond by saying: "Why don't you make a decision now so you can focus on your current needs?" Whatever the excuse or objection is, a professional salesperson never give up and keeps trying to reframe and translate these objections to opportunities.

 Rather than seeing objections as hindrances, they should be viewed and framed as opportunities.

Sometime objections are made before you even have the opportunity to discuss the project. This does not mean that you have to give up. Your prospect might say that they are too busy to talk about your product, do not give up, and keep pushing to reschedule to call them back. If they say they do not see how your product helps them, try to explain how your product helps them, and make sure you leave your contact information. At certain situations, prospects might ask you to send them information so they literally get rid of you, avoid the temptation to send such information and ask to meet them so you can tailor-make specific information to best meet their needs and fix their problems.

And one common objection is that many prospects would say that they already have a preferred vendor to deal with. If this happens, then, this is your golden opportunity to explain why the prospect has to look into other options and benchmark that vendor level of service, pricing, product quality and various other aspects to ensure their satisfaction is guaranteed, and how your product and company might help them achieve that. At the bottom of it, there must be something that you can find or exploit to get into a prospect business needs for which your product or service might offer an outstanding result.

2.4 Meet In The Middle

An essential part of the sales process is finding points of agreement with the prospect. By agreeing on small points, clients find it easier to agree to a sale. For example, a client who agrees that technical support after the sale is important may consider buying. You may also need to agree with a client's objection to close a sale. While trying to find points of agreement, focus on benefits, rather than just features. Each organization has its own set of features and benefits. Features are qualities of a product. A 4G phone is a feature. Benefits, on the other hand, solve problems, fill an emotional need, or make life easier for the customers. Sometimes features can become benefits. For example, a 4G phone provides the benefit of moving faster than the 3G models. Customers make purchases based on what they feel will benefit them personally. It is not enough to provide customers with a list of features; they need to see the benefits the features provide.

Then, figure out the unique selling position of your product or service. Every organization needs a unique selling position. This identifies how you are able to meet the needs of your target market. Your position has to be unique so that you can differentiate yourself from the competition, and it should motivate people to buy by solving a "pain point." A pain point is common need for consumers. It is important that your selling position be brief and to the point and typically a single sentence will do. There are basic steps to finding a unique sales position:

- List the basic benefits.
- Discover what makes them unique.
- Solve a pain point or performance gap.
- Condense your idea into a single sentence; offer proof of your product if you have it.
- You need to stand by your selling position. Be careful, and do not make promises you cannot keep.

If you define points of agreements and the unique selling position, and you still have some challenges or objections, and though it may seem counterintuitive, but sometimes the best way to make a sale is to agree with the customer's objections. By agreeing, you show the customer that you are listening and understand why he or she believes something. You use your agreement to educate the customer. Take the price objection, for example, rather than simply saying that the prices are high, explain why.

How to deal with a price objection?
"Yes, we do seem to be a little more expensive than some other companies, but we only use the highest quality material to create our products. We also offer a longer than average warranty, and customer support after the purchase with that price. Many organizations have an additional charge for customer support."

2.5 Give Them The Driving Wheel

It is important to understand that prospects, once voice out their concerns and objections, they may try to avoid a sale as they feel concerned about a price, benefit or any aspect as discussed earlier. Therefore, it is useful to have clients answer their own objections and have the driving wheel to lead the discussion. The questions that you ask about their concerns will show you how to move forward. A client who provides a reason for the objection is telling you what he or she needs to strike a deal and they are seeking for a clarification and an answer. A client who does not provide reasons for an objection is probably not focused on your conversation. Either way, the client's answer directs how you should proceed.

It is important to understand the problem that the client has with the objection. Price point is a common problem. Sometimes clients are simply trying to get a better deal and save money, and other times they honestly cannot afford your current price point. It is important to discover the difference by asking questions. Negotiation is part of any sales conversation, but you should only lower your price point when absolutely necessary, and do not reduce it too much or it will hamper the quality of your business. Before even you engage in price negotiations, you need to understand their target point and reasons for concerns.

Start asking questions such as; "why do you feel we are expensive? What price were you considering? Or what can you afford?" Price points are not the only objections clients should answer. Objections about the size or age of your company could indicate that they are afraid you cannot handle the job. Regardless of the objection, have clients answer so you know how to proceed.

Once you understand your client's problems with your business, you are able to reverse the objections and concerns. There are several ways to prove yourself and your company to your clients. Reinforce your expertise and carefully explain the logic behind your company's procedures and prices. Educate customers, particularly if you have addressed a problem already. Provide the background of the company along with its successes, explain why you are qualified to help, share case studies, statistics, and other evidence that prove your reason behind the price point... etc., and give the client testimonials from satisfied clients. Providing all of these might help overcome the customer concerns and give them confidence about your product, price and offerings.

> *When handling objections, you need to ask the right questions in order to develop a positive rapport; or touch the right nerve.*

2.6 Maintain Communication

The only way to overcome sales objections is to communicate with the client. You should already know to expect sales objections, concerns and questions, so bringing them up and discussing them with the client makes it easier for you to identify the inner workings and deflate objections. Sales people are familiar with certain objections. For example, those who work with higher end items should expect price objections. Rather than waiting for an objection, bringing it up first will disarm the prospect. By showing that you understand the common objections, the client will be more comfortable voicing more specific objections. For instance, you might start saying, "I know that we are a little more expensive than a few of our competitors, but please allow me to explain the quality of our product and service."

Finding the inner workings of an objection is similar to finding the customer's problem. The inner workings are voiced objections, and the way that they are worded indicate how deep the objections are and what you can do to address the needs of the client. By making it easy to voice objections, clients realize that you care about their individual needs. Nevertheless, you must realize that not every objection is voiced. There are different reasons why prospects do not voice every objection. They may be uncomfortable or they may feel that the sales representative will not understand. A well-trained sales representative will be able to uncover the unvoiced objections and address them to the client's satisfaction.

Prospects will provide clues to the real reason for the objection if you pay attention. Developing a relationship and communicating with clients will indicate if there are any unvoiced objections. Simply probe the client once you have developed a rapport, if you feel that he or she is holding back. You may wish to ask "Would you like to ask me anything at this point?" or "Can I answer any questions for you?" It is important to gently probe throughout the conversation until you are sure you have addressed every objection.

When you understand that the client has unspoken objections, it is important to bring them to light. Pay attention to reactions and notice when a client appears uncomfortable. Pay attention to their body language and whether it synchronizes correctly with their spoken words. Once you have identified the unspoken objections, you need to address them like you would any other personal objection. You may wish to say "Am I correct in thinking that you have a concern about what I just said?" or "Does this work for you?" Instead of asking, you may wish to start by offering some answers such as "Let me explain how this will increase your bottom line" or "With past clients, this has improved profits over time." By trying to reframe your understanding of their questions and offering answers, you would put your customers on ease and increase your chances to close a deal.

2.7 Follow The Process

There are five basic steps to handle all sales objections. It is important to never argue with clients about objections and follow this simple process. Rather, follow the basic steps to deal with objections and develop a strong working relationship with prospects.

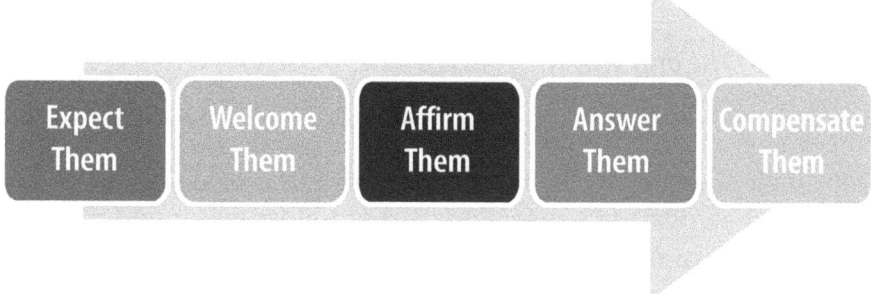

Figure 5 – *Five Steps To Handle Customers Concerns*

When it comes to sales objections, it is important to expect them. Allow customers to fully express their objections before you attempt to answer them. By expecting the sales objections, you will be better prepared to handle them when they do occur. Before you meet a potential customer, do your own research about their problems, and how your product will fix them, research what other products they purchased before, and how yours compare to theirs. Be ready with a list of questions you expect the customer would ask.

If you do your own research, then, you should not view sales objections as a hindrance to the sales process, instead, you have to welcome them. This tells you that the customer is showing some interest, as discussed earlier. Objections are an excellent sign. Customers do not voice certain objections unless they are interested in what you are presenting. Do not be annoyed and view objections as a customer's request for more information.

Then, you need to affirm the clients after they present their objections. Let them know that you understand their needs and want to answer their objections. You may also indicate that you have expected they might come up with these objections and you have done your own research on their problems to show how your products would fix them. This shows credibility and true intention to fix their problems and not only selling them. You can accomplish this by echoing the client and repeating what he says or rephrasing the objection as a question, which has been discussed earlier.

> **The only way to overcome sales objections is to communicate with the client.**

Once their objections are affirmed, you need to provide complete answers to the customer's objections. Do not gloss over questions and give vague answers, if you do not have answers, tell them that you will be getting back to them at later time. Prospects need facts, which help alleviate fear of taking a risk by doing business with you. If you do not have all of the pertinent information to answer their question, be honest and promise to contact them as soon as possible. For enterprise customers, you may need to provide some numbers, statistics, customer testimonials, past experiences or even a working prototype of your product.

Sometimes clients bring up objections that are legitimate problems. When this happens, you need to find a compensating benefit. For instance, your product might belong to a different price category than the majority of similar products in the marketplace, at this point, your customer might find your product super expensive, therefore, you have to offer them a compensating benefit such as; "I understand that this is cutting into your budget, but you will be able to save money over time because the quality of our merchandise means that you will not need to make as many orders as you do now." Another option would be to offer a more convenient payment plan, additional warranty or a discounted price for larger volumes. Try to ask your customer what makes them feel the price is comparable and which of the additional offerings they wish to consider.

2.8 Dos and Don'ts

There are some dos and don'ts to remember when handling sales objections. Most of the dos and don'ts are common sense. In the middle of a negotiation, however, it is easy to forget common sense rules. It is important to develop a rapport and earn the client's trust, so always remember the dos and don'ts. There are basic actions and behaviors you should always remember when you are handling sales objectives. Do:

- Stay positive.
- Listen carefully.
- Be aware of your body language.
- Affirm clients.
- Provide facts with your answers.

Additionally, there are some things that you should never do in a business meeting. In an effort to move past objections and close a deal, however, it is easy to forget the don'ts. Don't:

- Say something unflattering about your company.
- Say anything negative about the competition.
- Lose your temper.
- Lie, misrepresent or provide false information.
- Ignore an objection.

> *Customers do not voice certain objections unless they are interested in what you are presenting. Do not be annoyed and view objections as a customer's request for more information.*

2.9 Be Ready To Close

Once you overcome the sales objections, you should be able to seal the deal. Closing is a delicate process and it is critical to do it effectively. Time the close carefully, and practice tested and trusted closing techniques. Being over eager could cost you the sale. A common business acronym in deal closing is **ABC**, which stands for **Always Be Closing**.

The idea is that every conversation with a prospect is a chance to eventually close a sale. There are times, however, when it is more appropriate to ask a closing question then seal the deal. Customers provide clues in the way they interact with you. They will stop throwing out objections, and begin asking specific questions. For example they may ask about warranty or types of service after the sale. These indicate serious interest. After any presentation you should attempt a close with interested prospects. People who "think over" the sale rarely follow through.

There are different closing techniques that can be adapted for different situations or people such as asking a close question. A close question is designed to spur an action. We have all been asked close questions at retail stores, so they should be familiar. Regardless of the technique you use, close questions are involved. Once you ask a close question, wait for the customer to respond. All too often, sales representatives talk sales away. Silence is not bad for business. You may say "Would you like to take advantage of the special today or risk paying more in the future?"

Alternatively, you may wish to assume closing the deal. In this situation, you assume from the beginning that you will close the sale. You remain confident and approach the sale as doing the client a favor. You may wish to say, "I see that we are on the same page. Let's improve your product." You may also try taking physical action. Physical action closes involve doing something that helps the customer make the decision and introduces the closing question. For instance, you may wish to fill out an order form as you end the conversation, or ask the client to fill one out. And do not forget the best deal close. The best deal close should be familiar. We all hear them during sales events. This close appeals to the desire to save money or get something for nothing, such as "Today I can offer a 30 percent discount. I'm not sure how long this will last."

All of these techniques can be used to close a deal. However, it is always best to close when a client is on an emotional high and excited about the sale. Actually paying, however, can lead to emotional lows. In order to combat the emotional roller coaster, you need to reassure the customer about his or her decision. It is important to bring the emotions back up before making a closing statement. This is sometimes called "rollercoaster closing." There are a number of reasons to buy that give people a sense of security. Remind customers about these reasons to move the sale forward. You may wish to offer a money back guarantee so they are reassured of their purchase. You may wish to bring up again the different case studies and similar customers testimonials, and positive reviews by other similar customers. All of these would provide assurances to the customer before they make their purchase.

Finally, though it is your job to close a deal and push the customer to make a purchase, however, do not forget to remain calm and positive, this will help set the tone for the client. Do not pressure the customer and remember that no one likes feeling pressured. It is crucial not to forget offering reassurances and reasons to buy. Keep things simple to the customer and make the presentation easy to follow and always ask the closing question after addressing all concerns. By following these simple steps, you will be able to close as many deals as you plan.

Chapter 2 – Handling Sales Challenges

Q1- While walking around in the showroom, Mike noticed two couples examining the new car model his company introduced this year. Mike took this opportunity to talk to the couples about the car features, speed, gas mileage and others. For 20 minutes, Mike kept explaining what the new model is all offering. The couples eventually left without placing an order. What do you think Mike should have done differently?

- A- As people are naturally skeptical, and since this is a new car model, Mike should have asked questions and gathered more answers.
- B- As people are naturally skeptical, no matter what Mike does, the couples won't be buying.
- C- Mike should have rushed the presentation and pushed them to buy
- D- Mike should have overpromised and suggested they buy immediately

Q2- The three main reasons for customer concerns are:

- A- Overpricing, Overpromising, and rushing a deal
- B- Skepticism, misunderstanding and stalling
- C- Lack of features, pricing and warranties
- D- Agreement clauses and payment terms

Q3- This is the third presentation for ProductX that Steve is conducting for his client; Pam. Steve believes he addressed all Pam's questions, demonstrated several times ProductX and even deployed a trial version. Steve is unsure why Pam has not yet authorized the purchase!

- A- Steve should keep insisting that a purchase is done
- B- Steve may need to conduct a fourth product demo
- C- Steve needs to understand why ProductX is not meeting Pam's requirements
- D- Pam is possibly stalling as she is not the authorized person or is comparing various competitive products.

Q4- The best way for a salesperson to handle sales objectives is:

- A- To push them back to the potential client
- B- To consider them as opportunities
- C- To offer trials and product demos
- D- To keep presenting solutions and never quit

Q5- While conducting a product demo, Ashley was confronted with several questions, and failed to answer them up to the client satisfaction. What should Ashley have done?

- A- Ashely knows the product well, hence, she should have pointed that customer questions were wrong
- B- Ashley should have pointed that the customer did not understand how the product functions
- C- While being patient, Ashley could have argued why customers questions are irrelevant
- D- While showing respect, Ashley needs to park customer questions, and be better prepared next time.

Q6- To find the key selling position, the salesperson must focus on:

- A- Price
- B- Key benefits
- C- Key features
- D- After-sale services

Q7- If a customer asks: How old is your company? then they are basically concerned about:

- A- Pricing
- B- USP
- C- Aftersales support
- D- Capability to deliver the project

Q8- Usually, prospects will provide clues to the real reason for sales objection. Hence, the salesperson needs to focus on:

- A- Offering good pricing
- B- Building trust and relationship
- C- Explaining the USP
- D- Offer value add services

Q9- Denis feels his client has not shared their concerns about the product he is pushing to sell. What should Denis do?

- A- Go ahead and close the deal
- B- Ignore such concerns
- C- Bring them to light
- D- Offer trial version of the product to allow the client to test the product

Q10- The third step in handling customer concerns or sales objections is:

- A- Expect them
- B- Affirm them
- C- Answer them
- D- Compensate them

Answers

Q1- The correct answer is (A-As people are naturally skeptical, and since this is a new car model, Mike should have asked questions and gathered more answers).

Q2- The correct answer is (B-Skepticism, misunderstanding and stalling) and this primarily covers all other concerns

Q3- The correct answer is (D-Pam is possibly stalling as she is not the authorized person or is comparing various competitive products). Steve must have identified who the decision maker is from the beginning and inquire about potential competitors.

Q4- The correct answer is (B-To consider them as opportunities). Salesperson will not keep presenting if he realizes that he is talking to the wrong person or there is lack of seriousness or budget.

Q5- The correct answer is (D-While showing respect, Ashley needs to park customer questions, and be better prepared next time)

Q6- The correct answer is (B-Key benefits)

Q7- The correct answer is (D-Capability to deliver the project)

Q8- The correct answer is (B-Building trust and relationship) which is key to understand the real intentions and reasons of sales objections

Q9- The correct answer is (C-Bring them to light) and subsequently a solution is determined, whether it is to offer a trial product, demos or conducting any other activity.

Q10- The correct answer is (B-Affirm them)

EFFECTIVE PROPOSAL DEVELOPMENT

- What Is A Proposal?
- The Purpose Of The Proposal
- Proposal Framework
- Researching & Analysis
- Start Writing
- Generating Your First Draft
- Clarity & Readability
- Proofreading And Editing
- Make An Impression

Proposals are a very unique type of business documents. Salespersons create proposals to convey products or services features, benefits, prices, implementation methodology, service and warranty terms and other information to potential customers. There are developed to provide awareness and information to customers to help them make informed purchase decisions. Therefore, a good proposal does not just outline what product or service you would like to create or deliver, it does so in such a way that the reader feels it is the only logical choice for them to make, and hence, it helps you close a deal.

This chapter will discuss the proposal writing process, from understanding why you need to write a proposal; learning the various proposals types, analyzing your audience, gathering information; creating an outline and framework, writing, editing and proofreading; and creating the final and professional proposal document.

3.1 What Is A Proposal?

A proposal is primarily a sales pitch for a product or service that your company offers. It outlines a problem or opportunity that the client has and presents a product or service as a solution. This is a key point for salesperson to understand. Unless your proposal clearly show the customer how your product or service would fix their problem, ease their pain or increase their profits, then, your proposal and the efforts to create it go in vain.

Proposals can be directed externally to another organization or internally, for example, to senior management, in order to gain support for a project or idea. Proposals can also be solicited or unsolicited. Solicited proposals are written in response to a Request for Proposal (RFP) or Invitation for Proposal (IFP) issued by a customer. Unsolicited proposals are those that the organization sends on its own in an attempt to gain new business.

Writing proposals goes into several steps, and usually there are iterations and often these steps are repeated many times. This process will be discussed thoroughly in this chapter, however, before this is done, it is important to understand the various types of proposals first.

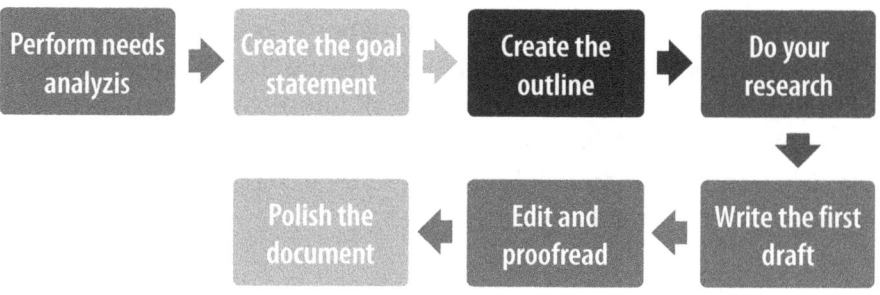

Figure 6 – *Proposal Writing Process*

There are four main categories of proposals, while these do overlap; each proposal is unique to each situation and each organization. A Technical Proposal is a specific kind of proposal that defines the technical requirements for a project. It also details the approach and complete plan including time, cost, and resources for the project. This proposal is excellent at showing companies how you can easily solve technological problems in their organization, without the need for them to find and hire skilled staff. Although these types of proposals are often read and approved by a technical team, it is important to include an executive summary, introduction, and conclusion that are written for the layman.

As you might imagine, Sales Proposals are usually written to convince a new client to purchase a product or service. This is done by building a case for why the client needs that particular product or service, and why you are the best person for the job. Because this type of proposal is essentially a sales pitch, clarity and conciseness are absolutely crucial. Make sure that this proposal focuses on what the solution can do for the customer, rather than the nuts and bolts of the proposed project.

> *Unless your proposal clearly show the customer how your product or service would fix their problem, ease their pain or increase their profits, then, your proposal and the efforts to create it go in vain.*

A Cost Proposal is an outline of estimated costs. It is usually prepared by a contractor to prepare for project negotiations. Usually, a cost proposal has solid estimates with backup data on the products or services being offered, with a detailed breakdown of all foreseeable costs, including material, resources, labor, equipment, travel, administrative expenses, etc. Since this proposal will be reviewed by executives, a summary of high-level costs should also be included.

The last type of proposals is a Professional Service proposal. It is a type of sales proposal that focuses on a professional service offering, such as public relations, marketing, or health care. Because of the focus on service, the proposal might have elements such as the list of the people who will be providing the service and their credentials, the organization's record of service, testimonials and references and resources available in the organization. You may also see some elements of the cost proposal, such as a breakdown of labor costs.

Earlier, It is mentioned that the proposal process can be initiated by a Request for Proposals (or RFP). This is a document issued by a company requesting proposals for a particular project. The RFP can be as simple or as detailed as a company likes, it all depends on what they require. Information commonly requested via an RFP can include:
- Organizational background
- Organization's experience with the requested product or service
- Solution details
- Project timeline and budget
- Customer references
- Resumes, product brochures, and many more

If you are responding to an RFP, always double and triple check that you have included all the information requested. If the RFP details a particular person to submit the proposal to, and a date to submit it by, follow their instructions. Any RFP requests (such as those pertaining to style, language, format, and/or template) should supersede any company or best-practice policies. If you are not sure which set of rules should take precedence, consult with your manager.

3.2 The Purpose Of The Proposal

To write a convincing proposal, you must get started on the right foot. This means that you have to determine the purpose of the proposal and gather background information about the customer need and problem. Your proposal should have a single goal in mind. What exactly will the proposal do? Is it convincing a customer to buy a specific product from you, hire you to do a service or renew an after sale contract. You need to find out that single goal. Then, identify who the audience will be. Is it the purchasing manager or the business team? It is crucial to know your audience so you specifically write to them in a language they understand and using terminology that relates to their business problem. To do so, it is important to perform a needs analysis. A good needs analysis must answer four questions:

1. Who are the customers of the proposal?
2. What do they want or need?
3. What do they currently have as a solution?
4. What can we offer?

To start, you should answer the first question. You may want to seek results from stakeholders or other interested parties. For example, if your senior management team has identified a sales opportunity, they may have some thoughts about possible customers. Keep an eye out for additional customer opportunities during the needs analysis process. Next, it is time to gather information about the customers. Stakeholders may be a possible source, as are market research studies, company reports, and organizational biographies. At times, you may be in contact with the customers themselves. Make use of open questions to gather as much information as possible. During the proposal writing, keep an eye out for new or changing answers to your needs analysis, and adjust your proposal approach as necessary.

Once the needs analysis is complete, it is time to write the goal statement. This will help you understand what you want to achieve. First, identify the type of proposal as per the fourth types discussed earlier. You may choose a type such as technical, sales, cost, or professional service, or it may be of a different type altogether, such as a non-profit grant proposal. In general, the writing process remains the same irrespective of the type of the proposal, which usually relates to the differences of the content itself. Next, add in the purpose of your proposal. Finally, bring it all together into the goal statement. This statement typically looks like the following: "Our *technical proposal* will convince the customer *to upgrade to our XYZ Health product.*"

> *There are four main categories of proposals; these are technical, sales, cost and professional services proposals.*

3.3 Proposal Framework

Now that we have our background information, it is time to start creating the framework for the proposal. The preparation process could be simple or detailed, however, the more detailed and accurate your outline is the more cohesive and persuasive your proposal will be. With that being said, the outline should not be set in stone, it must evolve as the proposal is being built.

Proposals vary widely in their size and structure. However, most proposals include the following elements, listed in the order that they typically appear in the proposal:

1. **Cover Letter**: Like a resume cover letter, this document outlines what your company is, the basic thrust of the proposal, and any conditions, such as a date of expiry. It should be signed by your senior officers.

2. **Title Page**: Every proposal should have a title. The title page should include the title, the client's name, and address, the name of the person receiving the proposal, your company's name, and address, and the date the proposal will be submitted. If you are responding to a request for proposal (RFP), the first line of

the title page should say, "Response to Requirements," and the proposal number should be listed below the title.

3. **Proprietary Notice**: It is always a good idea to outline how the information in the proposal can and cannot be used, shared, and transmitted. Get your legal team's help with this section.

4. **Table of Contents**: A list of all the major sections and sub-sections in your proposal. You can use Arabic or Roman numerals; just be consistent and note that most word processors can generate this for you automatically.

5. **Executive Summary**: This is the most important selling tool in your proposal. It should be aimed at the executives in the client's organization. It should outline the proposed solution, why the solution was chosen, project management details, how the product will be handed off to the organization if appropriate, major benefits that will be realized, high-level cost and time estimates, and why your organization is the best candidate for the task. This summary must be no longer than two pages at max.

6. **Introduction**: An explanation of why you are writing the proposal, and an overview of what to expect. In this section, you may wish also to include an explanation of *your* understanding of the customer requirements, or what we call a 'Statement Of Understanding'. This demonstrates to the customer that your solution aims to solve problems as explained in your understanding section, and gives them the opportunity to verify it. If there were any discrepancies, the customer would come forward and clarify these for you.

7. **Body**: The meat of the proposal, organized by headings, your major points, and sub-headings. This body might also be structured into technical vs. commercial sections.

8. **Summary and Conclusions**: Summarize the main points covered, the proposed solution, and why your organization is the best candidate for the task.

9. **Bibliography**: List of resources used in the proposal.

10. **Appendices**: List of additional information that deems to be useful but does not warrant to be used as part of the body. This could include your resources resumes, additional product images or marketing materials.

In addition to the standard components, here are some optional components that you might see in a proposal:

- Table of Figures
- Statement of understanding
- Organizational history
- Summary of writer's credentials
- Proposed project timeline
- Cost-benefit analysis
- Benefits summary
- Scientific method
- Budget and payment terms
- Specific project elements, such as proposed product design, marketing plan, schedule, etc.
- Problem analysis
- Glossary of jargon, technical terms, etc.

Once the standard components and any special sections are outlined, it is time to build the body of your proposal. To start, outline the major points that your proposal will contain. Remember, this is just the starting point and serves as a guideline, you can move sections around and add additional points as you perform your research and write the proposal. Once you have your main points outlined, add the supporting or sub-points beneath each heading. It is recommended to have at least two sub-points and a maximum of nine per heading. If you can not find two sub-points, you may want to combine that major heading with another one. By finishing this, you will have your outline and proposal framework ready.

 Before jumping in writing your proposal, determine its purpose and gather background information about the customer need and problem.

3.4 Researching & Analysis

Now that we have an outline built, it is time to find resources, facts and information to support your headings and sub-headings in the proposal. There are various resources to use to build your proposal. You may gather information from your company employees, documents and reports. You may also consult with industry experts and technical magazines. You may also observe and interview potential customers or how existing customers use your products or other competitor products to get some insights. Always get the original documentation. For example, if an employee gives you statistics from last year's financial statement, you have to gather a copy of the statement yourself and verify the statistics. Make sure to properly source the documentation in your report.

The Internet can be an excellent resource for gathering information if it is used properly. You need to make sure that the information you gather is reliable and credible. You may only use information from accredited, reliable organizations such as the government, major non-profit organizations, and accredited institutions. You have to always go directly to the source to get your information. For example, if you find a blog that references an interesting study, track down the study and use its information during your proposal. You may need to contact an organization by phone or e-mail to get the report that you need. Finally, remember that your outline is just a guideline, if you find additional information that you feel is pertinent, review the outline to see where it can be included, and revise as necessary.

Information should, naturally, be organized by heading and sub-heading. Within those groupings, however, there are some other ways to organize information. The most common choice for a proposal is from problem to solution. This means that a sub-heading section would start with a problem statement, spend several paragraphs outlining the options, making your organization's offering seem the most attractive, and offer a conclusion at the end. Nonetheless, you may consider some other methods such as:

- Chronological order (most recent to oldest, or vice versa)
- By level of detail (simplest to most complex, or vice versa)
- By importance (high, medium, low)
- Separated by pros and cons, with a conclusion at the end
- By offering a question and then an answer

3.5 Start Writing

The research is done, the outline is complete, and you are ready to write, right? Hold on just a moment! Before you dive into your word processor, you have to keep an eye on some basic writing skills. Paying attention to proper spelling and grammar is general good practice, and it will make your editing process a lot easier. Although you do not need to worry about perfection at this point, it is worthwhile to keep some basic spelling and grammar tips in mind. For instance, proposals should usually use the third person (it, they), or rarely the second person (we). Never use the first person (I, me, she, and he). Also, acronyms and texting slang do not belong in a proposal, or in any business document, for that matter. Additionally, know what errors you commonly make so that you can make an effort to correct them. Once writing, make use of available tools, such as spell check, dictionaries, thesauri, and people directories. And finally, always re-read your work; have someone else read it too, if possible.

 You need to make sure that the information you gather is reliable and credible.

Choosing the correct word can make the difference between comprehension and confusion. Take the time to make sure your words reflect what you really want to say. Proposals should be objective rather than subjective. This means that you have to leave your opinions out! For example, instead of saying, "Last year's numbers were abysmal," give the exact statistic and let the reader draw their own conclusion. You need to include the appropriate level of detail in each sentence and paragraph. Too little detail will leave the reader confused; too much detail and they may become bored. Remember, this is where a good understanding of your audience comes in handy. Also, check to see if you have said the same thing in different ways, this will help make your writing as concise as possible. To see if you have used the right word, try substituting synonyms for your chosen word, for example, you may wish to use 'fair', 'reasonable' and 'just' interchangeably. In technical proposals, you may have to use technical acronyms or jargons, ensure you provide a glossary to explain their meanings.

In general, when writing sentences and paragraphs, keep them as short as possible; ten to fifteen words is the optimum length. If you have used "and" or "but," or punctuation such as a comma or semicolon, see if you can break the sentence up. Peoples' attention spans are getting shorter every day, meaning they are more likely to read short paragraphs with short, easy to read sentences. When writing paragraphs, you have to stick to its structure of a beginning, middle and an end. Each paragraph focuses on one theme or idea and it ties to the paragraphs before and after it to help build to a logical conclusion. Overall, you have to maintain consistency in your writing, make sure your proposal is sending a clear, consistent message.

While writing, try to provide testimonials or examples of how other customers have used your products or services. This is called 'Social Validation'; people tend to follow the crowd. If possible, show how elements in your proposal were successful for people known to the proposal audience. Be friendly in your proposal. You will not win by badgering, bullying, or insulting. Be direct, and establish why you are the experts in this area, and why you are the right people to be making this proposal. Finally, your clients would love to get something special so they feel compelled to give back, like a special offer specifically tailored to them. If you know your audience well, your proposal should speak and address them and their need directly, consistently and friendly.

3.6 Generating Your First Draft

It is finally time to generate your first draft. The importance of a draft is it allows you to assess how the reader or evaluator would think of your proposal and offers you the chance to rewrite some of its sentences, clarify some numbers or revise its outline. While writing your proposal, always ask yourself: what will the person reading this proposal receive from this sentence/paragraph/section? After all, your audience must be able to understand your proposal to approve it!

To help your audience understand your proposal, you may provide a Statement of Understanding. This is an optional section of the proposal, but it is very useful if you are presenting a proposal to solve a client's problem. This section contains a statement reflecting your understanding of the problem. This is a great opportunity to show that you have done your research about the client's business and that you understand their needs. You may wish to include a Benefits Analysis. This section will highlight the advantages to the reader if they approve your proposal. If appropriate, costs for each benefit can be included. Just make sure you have some solid numbers to offer, and communicate that this is an analysis only and not a guarantee of results.

Other proposals might also include an Organizational Impact Statement. This section can be used to outline the impact on the client's organization by using your products or services. This is an excellent section to outline "soft" or intangible benefits if you have included a cost-benefit analysis such as; improved customer confidence, alignment with industry standards or process standardization and improvement.

When writing the proposal, make sure to include alternate solutions, and to show why they are not appropriate. This is called Ghosting. Whenever possible, highlight the deficiencies in other approaches to the problem, and how your proposed solution does not have those areas of weakness. For maximum impact, structure this analysis in terms of risk mitigation and maximum benefit for the client reading the proposal. While you are ghosting, do not forget to include your own company. Point out where possible weaknesses or problems can occur; especially if they are well known, and why these issues will not be a concern for the client.

A powerful element of your proposal is using of pictures and illustrations. A picture is worth a thousand words, if it is done correctly. Therefore, you may use an illustration if it helps to convey your point and make the illustration simple and convey one major point. Some information are best presented using charts or diagrams, and not images, hence, you have to pick your illustration wisely. Finally, if your proposal includes many illustrations, number each sequentially and include a Table of Figures at the beginning of your proposal.

3.7 Clarity & Readability

Once your proposal is written, it is time to check it for clarity and readability. You need to verify your use of words, their correct meaning and whether you have used them on their right context. What about punctuation! And use of jargons or technical acronyms! Have you provided a glossary for those? You need to revisit your sentences, paragraphs and whether you used an active or passive voice. Is there a logical sequence in your paragraphs and does each paragraph have a logical beginning, middle, and end, focused around one idea? Does each paragraph, sub-section, and section tie back to the goal statement?

An important aspect to check while verifying your proposal for clarity is trying to anticipate what questions your audience might have while reading your proposal, and work your way out to answer these in the proposal itself. For instance, have you provided a glossary for specific acronyms, have you written at an appropriate level? Are all sections written for the correct audience? For example, if you have written a technical proposal, the body may be written for a technical audience, while the executive summary may be written at a higher level. Have you provided enough background information? Do your supporting points clearly lead to a conclusion? If at all possible, have someone similar to your audience read your proposal and highlight areas that need clarification.

> *Use Social Validation by providing testimonials or examples of how other customers have used your products or services.*

Finally, if you have verified your proposal and believe it is ready, you may wish to include the Gunning Fog Index. The index takes a sample of writing, performs calculations on it, and outputs the level of education, for example, Grade 9 that a person will theoretically need to read it. Most business documents, including proposals, should be written at a grade eight or nine level. This helps in clarifying any complex concepts or acronyms using a much simpler language. There are several software applications that would help you calculate the index for your proposal and offer advices on optimizing it.

3.8 Proofreading And Editing

With all the hard work you have put into your proposal, the last thing you want is for it to be tossed into a corner because of problems with the presentation or spelling and grammar errors. Even if someone else will be editing your work, you should always proofread and edit your writing before handing it off. This way, you can make sure that you said what you really meant to say. You need to focus on both editing and proofreading. Editing is different from proofreading in that proofreading mainly focuses on spelling and grammar, while editing looks at the clarity, accuracy, and consistency of the document as a whole.

When people read a document, they do not read every word. Instead, their minds scan each sentence to gain overall comprehension. This makes it tough to spot and correct errors. Therefore, you may wish to take extra measures to proofread your proposal. For instance, you need to set up an environment conducive to editing, with good lighting, minimal distractions, and all the tools you need. While reading, make a conscious effort to read slowly and try to read the document several times and loud, while sometimes, you may read in opposite order, i.e. from the bottom to the top of the page, and from the end to the beginning of a paragraph. If you are not sure what a word means, or if it has been used correctly or not, look it up in the glossary to verify it is there.

An effective technique to use to proofread and edit your proposal is peer review. In a peer review setting, the editor notes recommended changes and then hands the document back to the writer for revision, so make sure your editing marks are clear. Electronic review may be particularly useful if there are multiple reviewers. During reviews, peers might also verify the facts that are presented in the proposal. They validate quotes from people, mathematical calculations, presentation, analysis, and interpretation of studies, phrasing of statistics; for example, use of words like always, exactly, never, and many more. The fact checking must also ensure that first-hand information is available. For example, if a scientific study is quoted, that study must be available, not another item such as a newspaper article quoting it.

Peer review should be a mandatory component of any proposal writing process. Typically, your peer editor reviews the document, and then gives you feedback to incorporate into the proposal. Why is peer review so important? First, because of the way the human brain works, it is physically impossible for you to see many of your own errors. Second, having someone else read your work will help ensure that you have included all points to make a logical, clear case. Third, everyone has their personal areas of writing weaknesses, and peer review will help compensate for those weaknesses.

3.9 Make An Impression

Your proposal has been thoroughly researched, brilliantly written, and carefully edited. But it is the presentation that truly matters and will grant the first great impression, otherwise, all of your hard work will likely go unnoticed. You have to present your proposal in a professional way, by selecting the right formats, fonts, styles, structure and many more.

When preparing your proposal, remember that less is more. First and foremost, respect company policies and any requirements set out by the client. Their rules supersede anything you may read here. When using fonts, use a maximum of two font faces, one for headings and one for the body and use common fonts, such as Times New Roman, Calibri, Arial, or Verdana. If you use font effects, use them sparingly, and stick to the basic effects (bold, italic, and underline). If your word processor offers a consistent way to use formatting (such as styles or themes), make use of it, instead of creating your own. When formatting your proposal, establish a consistent formatting scheme throughout the document.

In addition to clean, consistent fonts, there are a few other things that you can do to give your proposal that extra touch. Give your proposal a title and create a title page. If the document contains signatures, get everyone to sign in the same color ink and you may use the same pen if possible. Maintain consistency when using headers and footers, and always include page numbers to allow easier referencing at later stage and ensure all components, headers, footers, illustrations, text, cover pages, etc., match.

If your proposal is ready, all proofreading, editing, peer reviews, presentation editing is done, then, you may have to print it to be delivered to your client. If this is the case, you will want to make sure that its appearance reflects all the hard work put into it. If there are illustrations and use of color is crucial, then, print the proposal in color and good quality white paper, with dark blue or black type. Make sure that all sections are present and that all pages are in order. Use simple and professional binding, such as spiral binding or an elegant three-ring binder can make a big impact.

 Use Gunning Fog Index to ensure your writing is adequate for the majority of your audience.

If you wish to provide a soft copy of your proposal, you may include a disc or a USB drive that includes an electronic copy of the proposal and any key documents can be added to the paper copy. Make sure to keep printed copies clean and dry. If, after the printout, corrections need to be made, make them in the word processor and print new copies. You can also create an errata sheet and add it to the beginning of the proposal. If you are mailing the proposal, use a manila or padded envelope big enough to contain the proposal, without folding it. Spend the extra money to courier it, rather than tossing it in the mail. If it is to be e-mailed, choose a commonly used format, such as PDF. Make sure the file is small enough to be transmitted to all parties. Be sure to include a subject line and brief note, or even the cover letter, in the body. By following these simple tips, you will make a great first impression for your proposal.

Chapter 3 – Effective Proposal Development

Q1- The first step in the proposal writing process is:
- A- Create goal statement
- B- Create outline
- C- Proofread
- D- Perform needs analysis

Q2- _____ **outlines what your company is, the basic thrust of the proposal, and any conditions, such as a date of expiry.**
- A- Title page
- B- RFP
- C- Cover Letter
- D- Proprietary Notice

Q3- RFP is an important document in the procurement process, and usually generated by:
- A- Suppliers to respond to customers
- B- Customers to service providers
- C- Prepared jointly
- D- Prepared by third party

Q4- Examples of how other customers have used your products or services are important because they offer:
- A- Testimonials
- B- Social Validation
- C- Publicity
- D- Market Value

Q5- When writing the proposal, you may include alternate solutions to show why they are not appropriate, and your solution is superior is called:
- A- Competitive Comparison
- B- Ghosting
- C- Comparable solutions
- D- Alternatives

Q6- Bill has approved the implementation of a new product offered by your company. To make sure that it fits Bill company, Bill needs to conduct:

- A- Market Research
- B- Brainstorming
- C- Organizational Impact Assessment
- D- Risk Analysis

Q7- In writing proposals, you should never use:

- A- Third person
- B- Second person
- C- First person
- D- Fourth person

Q8- In drafting your proposal, the most important section is:

- A- Pricing
- B- Introduction
- C- Executive Summary
- D- Body

Q9- Usually, public relations, marketing, or health care proposals are called:

- A- Cost Proposals
- B- Professional Service Proposals
- C- Sales Proposals
- D- Technical Proposal

Q10- In proposal development, IFP stands for:

- A- Information for Proposal
- B- Invitation for Planning
- C- Invitation for Proposal
- D- Information for Planning

Answers

Q1- The correct answer is (D-Perform needs analysis)

Q2- The correct answer is (C-Cover Letter)

Q3- The correct answer is (B-Customers to service providers)

Q4- The correct answer is (B-Social Validation) is the ultimate goal of testimonials.

Q5- The correct answer is (B-Ghosting)

Q6- The correct answer is (C-Organizational Impact Assessment)

Q7- The correct answer is (C-First Person) such as (I, me, she and he).

Q8- The correct answer is (C-Executive Summary)

Q9- The correct answer is (B-Professional Service Proposals)

Q10- The correct answer is (C-Invitation for Proposal)

CHAPTER 4

EFFECTIVE COMMUNICATION STRATEGIES

- Defining Communication
- Understanding Communication Barriers
- It Is Not What You Say
- Non-Verbal Communication
- Speaking Like A STAR
- Listening Skills
- Probing Skills
- Conversation Framework
- Feelings & Communication

F or the better part of every day, we are communicating to and with others. Whether it is the speech you deliver in the boardroom, the level of attention you give your spouse when they are talking to you, or the look that you give to the cat, it all means something. As an effective leader, manager or employee, you have to learn how to communicate effectively, master oral and written communication, verbal and non-verbal, and use different methods and communication styles.

4.1 Defining Communication

For many people, communication refers to the spoken word, people who are hearing impaired, however, might think of sign language and people who are visually impaired might think of Braille as well as sounds and they consider it all as communication. Communication is *"the imparting or interchange of thoughts, opinions, or information by speech, writing, or signs."* It is also defined as *"means of sending messages, orders, etc., including telephone, telegraph, radio, and television"*. No matter what definition you choose, communication entails sending and receiving messages, between two or many parties, and happens within a context. Basically, we communicate in three major ways:

- **Spoken:** There are two components to spoken communication; verbal or what you are saying and paraverbal which means how you say it; your tone, speed, pitch, and volume.
- **Non-Verbal:** These are the gestures and body language that accompany your words, such as arms folded across your chest, tracing circles in the air, tapping your feet, or having a hunched-over posture.
- **Written:** Communication can also take place via fax, e-mail, or written words.

In addition to how we communicate, the method in which the communicator shares his or her message is important as it has an effect on the message itself. Communication methods include person-to-person, telephone, e-mail, fax, radio, public presentation, television broadcast, and many more! The person or people receiving the message affect the message, too. Their understanding of the topic and the way in which they receive the message can affect how it is interpreted and understood.

4.2 Understanding Communication Barriers

On the surface, communication seems pretty simple. I talk and you listen. You send me an e-mail and I read it. Like most things in life, however, communication is far more complicated than it seems and can be easily impacted by several barriers. These barriers typically break down into three categories: language, culture, and location barriers.

Of course, one of the biggest barriers to written and spoken communication is language. If the people who are communicating speak different languages, then, there is none or little grounds for common understanding, or if the language being used is not the first language for one or more people involved in the communication. In some cases, people might speak the same language but might have different dialects and or unique subtleties. This will also impede the effectiveness of communications, and might eventually lead to conflicts.

There are a few ways to reduce the impact of language communication barriers.
- *As a group, identify that the barrier exists. Identify things that the group can do to minimize it.*
- *Pictures speak a thousand words, and can communicate across languages.*
- *If you are going to be communicating with this person on a long-term basis, try to find a common language or you may also consider hiring a translator.*

There can also be times when people speak the same language, but are from a different culture, where different words or gestures can mean different things. Or, perhaps the person you are communicating with is from a different class from you, or has a very different lifestyle.

All of these things can hinder your ability to get your message across effectively.

If you have the opportunity to prepare, find out as much as you can about the other person's culture and background, and how it differs from yours. Try to identify possible areas of misunderstanding and how to prevent or resolve those problems. If you do not have time to prepare, and find yourself in an awkward situation, use the cultural differences to your advantage. Ask about the differences that you notice, and encourage questions about your culture. Ensure that your questions are curious, not judgmental, resentful, or otherwise negative.

The last barrier is location, defined by time and place. These barriers often occur when people are in different time zones or different places. Ignoring the existence of location barriers can lead to missed deadlines or confusions on rooms or venues reservations. If you are scheduling a conference call with overseas teams, make it clear what time zone the meeting time is booked against. It does worth to spend few minutes at the first of any orientation session or kickoff meeting to acknowledge that you have team members from different time zones and educate everyone on the differences. With little planning and awareness, location barriers can be easily overcome.

Another thing to watch out for is rushed communication. The pressure of time can cause either party to make assumptions and leaps of faith. Always make sure you communicate as clearly as possible, and ask for playback. Once assumptions are defined, always validate and verify every assumption with your team members. Communication has to be planned, hence, ensure your activity list includes specific tasks to schedule meetings, preparing agenda, meeting people, documenting reports and presenting these reports on a timely manner, so you avoid the last minute rush.

4.3 It Is Not What You Say

Have you ever heard the saying, "*It is not what you say, it is how you say it*"? Indeed, It is true! How you say your messages is called paraverbal communication; which is the message told through the pitch, tone, and speed of our words when we communicate.

Pitch can be most simply defined as the key of your voice. A high pitch is often interpreted as anxious or upset. A low pitch sounds more serious and authoritative. People will pick up on the pitch of your voice and react to it. As well, variation in the pitch of your voice is important to keep the other party interested. If you naturally speak in a very high-pitched or low-pitched voice, work on varying your pitch to encompass all ranges of your vocal cords. One easy way to do this is to relax your throat when speaking. Make sure to pay attention to your body when doing this as you do not want to damage your vocal cords.

The combination of various pitches to influence an audience is very effective if managed carefully. Many leaders emphasize the 'I' with louder pitch once they want to get an audience attention to their achievements and they wanted to clearly related these achievements to them and only them. This is why you would see them say loud and clear and with emphasis to deliver a positive and authoritative tone.

The pace at which you speak also has a tremendous effect on your communication ability. From a practical perspective, someone who speaks quickly is harder to understand than someone who speaks at a moderate pace. Conversely, someone who speaks very slowly will probably lose their audience interest before they get very far! A hurried pace can make the listener feel anxious and rushed whereas a slow pace can make the listener feel as though your message is not important. A moderate pace will seem natural, and will help the listener focus on your message.

One easy way to check your pitch, tone, and speed is to record yourself speaking. Think of how you would feel listening to your own voice and work on speaking the way you would like to be spoken to.

4.4 Non-Verbal Communication

When you are communicating, your body is also communicating and sending a message that is as powerful as your words, if not more powerful. Though body language interpretations are common, nonetheless body language can also mean different things across different genders and cultures. For instance, a person sitting with his or her legs crossed may simply be more comfortable that way, and not necessarily feeling closed-minded towards a specific discussion, as would a common inter-pretation for his body language might suggest. However, it is good to understand how various behaviors are often seen, so that we can make sure our body is sending the same message as our mouth. To become an effective communicator, you have to understand how to use your body language effectively.

In 1971, psychologist Albert Mehrabian published a famous study called *Silent Messages*. In it, he made several conclusions about the way the spoken word is received. Although this study has been misquoted often throughout the years, its basic conclusion is that 7% of our message is verbal, 38% is paraverbal, and 55% is from body language. Now, we know this is not true in all situations. If someone is speaking to you in a foreign language, you cannot understand 93% of what they are saying or if you are reading a written letter, you are likely getting more than 7% of the sender's message. What this study does tell us is that body language is a vital part of our communication with others; it is the way in which our body speaks to others.

There are different body signs that send different meanings to an audi-ence. The way we stand or sit, the positions of our arms, legs, feet and hands, facial expressions and gestures are all body signs that carry dif-ferent meanings.

Common interpretations for body language:
- *Sitting hunched over typically indicates stress or discomfort.*
- *Leaning back when standing or sitting indicates a casual and relaxed demeanor.*
- *Standing ramrod straight typically indicates stiffness and anxiety.*
- *Crossed arms and legs often indicate a closed mind.*
- *Fidgeting is usually a sign of boredom or nervousness.*
- *Smiles and frowns speak a million words.*
- *A raised eyebrow can mean inquisitiveness, curiosity, or disbelief.*
- *Chewing one's lips can indicate thinking, or it can be a sign of boredom, anxiety, or nervousness.*

As an effective communicator, you have to interpret body language and gestures carefully. A gesture is a non-verbal message that is made with a specific part of the body. Gestures differ greatly from region to region, and from culture to culture. While nodding head gesture is considered a positive acknowledgement in one culture, it means the opposite in another culture. As effective communicator, you have to be culturally sensitive when it comes to interpreting gestures.

Common gestures interpretations in North America			
Gesture	**Interpretation**	**Gesture**	**Interpretation**
Nodding head	Yes	Thumbs down	Disagreement, not OK
Shaking head	No	Pointing index finger	Indicating, blaming
Moving head from side to side	Maybe	Handshake	Welcome, introduction
Shrugging shoulders	Not sure; I don't know	Flap of the hand	Does not matter, go ahead
Crossed arms	Defensive	Waving hand	Hello
Tapping hands or fingers	Bored, anxious, nervous	Waving both hands over head	Help, attention
Shaking index finger	Angry	Crossed legs or ankles	Defensive
Thumbs up	Agreement, OK	Tapping toes or feet	Bored, anxious, nervous

4.5 Speaking Like A STAR

While talking to an audience, you have to ensure the messages are clear, complete, correct, and concise, with the **STAR** communication model. STAR model refers to Situation, Task, Action and Result. First, state what the situation is. Try to make this no longer than one sentence. If you are having trouble, ask yourself, "Where?", "Who?", and, "When?", this will provide a base for the message so it can be clear and concise.

Next, briefly state what your task is. Again, this should be no longer than one sentence. Use the question, "What?" to frame your sentence, and add the "Why?" if appropriate. Now, state what you did to resolve the problem in one sentence. Use the question, "How?" to frame this part of the statement. The Action part will provide a solid description and state the precise actions that will resolve any issues. And finally, state what the result was. This will often use a combination of the six W's question types; What, Who, When, Where, Why and How. Again, a precise short description of the results that come about from your previous steps will finish on a strong definite note.

Try this example to see how to use STAR communication model to communicate effectively to an audience.

Situation = "On Tuesday, I was in a director's meeting at the main plant."

Task = "I was asked to present last year's sales figures to the group."

Action = "I pulled out my laptop, fired up PowerPoint, and presented my slide show."

Result = "Everyone was wowed by my prep work, and by our great figures!"

4.6 Listening Skills

So far, we have discussed all the components of sending a message effectively using nonverbal, paraverbal, and verbal means. It is also quite crucial to effectively receive messages in a cycle of communication. For most of us, our body does the hearing by interpreting the sounds that we hear into words. Listening, however, is far more difficult. Listening is the process of looking at the words and the other factors around the words; such as our non-verbal communication, and then interpreting the entire message.

To become a better listener, you have to make serious to improve your listening skills. When you are listening, you have to literary listen. Do not talk on the phone, text message, clean off your desk, or do anything else. This also requires that you avoid interruptions. If you think of something that needs to be done, make a mental or written note of it and forget about it until the conversation is over. Also, when you do talk, make sure it is related to what the other person is saying. Ask questions to clarify, expand, and probe for more information. While listening, If you are not sure what the other party wants, just ask!

Another important element to effective listening is the physical environment. Try to reduce noise and distractions. If possible, be seated comfortably and be close enough to the person so that you can hear them, but not too close to make them uncomfortable. Finally, If it is a conversation where you are required to take notes, try not to let the note-taking disturb the flow of the conversation, instead, use a sound recorder so you can transcript the notes later. If you need a moment to catch up, choose an appropriate moment to ask for a break.

There is another element to listening, which is active listening. Active listening goes above and beyond effective listening by truly understanding the meaning and background of what is being said. As an active listener, you have to identify where the other person is coming from. This concept is also called the frame of reference. For example, your reaction to a bear will be very different if you are viewing it in a zoo, or from your tent at a campsite. Your approach to someone talking about a sick relative will differ depending on their relationship with that person. You have to listen to what is being said closely and attentively and if you do so, you will be able to respond appropriately, either non-verbally, such as a nod to indicate you are listening, with a question, to ask for clarification, or by paraphrasing. Note that paraphrasing does not mean repeating the speaker's words back to them like a parrot. It does mean repeating what you think the speaker said in your own words.

> *Paraphrasing does not mean repeating the speaker's words back to them like a parrot. It does mean repeating what you think the speaker said in your own words.*

When we are listening to others speak, there are three kinds of cues that we can give the other person. Using the right kind of cue at the right time is crucial for keeping good communication going. The three kinds of cues are:

- **Non-Verbal**: As shown in the Mehrabian study, body language plays an important part in our communications with others. Head nods and an interested facial expression will show the speaker that you are listening.
- **Quasi-Verbal**: Fillers words like, "uh-huh," and "mm-hmmm," show the speaker that you are awake and interested in the conversation.
- **Verbal**: Asking open questions using the six roots discussed earlier (who, what, where, when, why, how), paraphrasing, and asking summary questions are all key tools for active listening.

These cues should be used as part of active listening. Inserting an occasional "uh-huh," during a conversation may fool the person that you are communicating with in the short term, but you are fooling yourself if you feel that this is an effective communication approach.

4.7 Probing Skills

Good questioning and probing skills are another building block of successful communication. Questions would help us gather information, clarify facts, and communicate with others. As an effective communicator, you have to ask open or closed questions to seek clarification, completeness and correctness, determining information relevance, drilling down on information or summarizing.

Open questions get their name because the response is open-ended; the answerer has a wide range of options to choose from when answering it. Open questions use one of six words as a root: Who? What? Where? When? Why? And How? Open questions are like going fishing with a net, you never know what you are going to get! Open questions are great conversation starters, fact finders, and communication enhancers.

Closed questions are the opposite of open questions; their very structure limits the answer to yes or no, or a specific piece of information. Some examples include: Do you approve funding the new project? Or Have you hired the new analyst? Although closed questions tend to shut down communication, they can be useful if you are searching for a particular piece of information, or winding a conversation down. If you use a closed question and it shuts down the conversation, simply use an open-ended question to get things started again.

In addition to the basic open and closed questions, there is also a toolbox of probing questions that we can use. These questions can be open or closed, but each type serves a specific purpose. You can probe for clarification. You invite the other person to share more information so that you can fully understand their message. Another type of probing questions is for seeking completeness and correctness of information or stories. These types of questions can help you ensure you have the full, true story. Having all the facts, in turn, can protect you from assuming and jumping to conclusions.

If you want to confirm relevance of certain information, then, you probe information on this regard. This category will help you determine how or if a particular point is related to the conversation at hand. It can also help you get the speaker back on track from a tangent. You might wish to drill down on a specific issue and to nail vague statements before forming your ideas. And finally, you probe questions that would help summarize a situation or a case. These questions are framed more like a statement. They pull together all the relevant points. They can be used to confirm to the listener that you heard what was said, and to give them an opportunity to correct any misunderstandings. Be careful not to avoid repeating the speaker's words back to them like a parrot.

Remember, paraphrasing means repeating what you think the speaker said in your own words.

4.8 Conversation Framework

Engaging in interesting, memorable small talk is a daunting task for most people. How do you know what to share and when to share it? How do you know what topics to avoid? How do you become an engaging converser? Most experts propose a simple three-level framework that you can use to master the art of conversation. Identifying where you are and where you should be is not always easy, but having an objective outline can help you stay out of sticky situations. The conversation framework has three steps:

- First step is focused on discussing general topics.
- Second step is focused on sharing ideas and perspectives.
- Third step is focused on sharing personal experiences

Step One: Discussing General Topics

At the most basic level, you have to stick to general topics: the weather, sports, non-controversial world events, movies, and books. This is typically what people refer to when they say, "small talk." At this stage, you will focus on facts rather than feelings, ideas, and perspectives. Death, religion, and politics are absolute no-no's. The exception is when you know someone has had an illness or death in the family and wish to express condolences. In this situation, keep your condolences sincere, brief, and to the point.

If someone shares a fact that you feel is not true, try to refrain from pointing out the discrepancy. If you are asked about the fact, it is ok simply to say, "I was not aware of that," or make some other neutral comment. Right now, you are simply getting to know the other party. Keep an eye out for common ground while you are communicating and use open-ended questions and listening skills to get as much out of the conversation as possible.

Step Two: Sharing Ideas and Perspectives

If the first level of conversation goes well, the parties should feel comfortable with each other and have identified some common ground.

Now it is time to move a bit beyond general facts and share different ideas and perspectives. It is important to note that not all personal experiences are appropriate to share at this level.

Although this level of conversation is the one most often used, and is the most conducive to relationship building and opening communication channels, make sure that you do not limit yourself to one person in a large social gathering. It is useful mingle successfully with your network or other employees.

Step Three: Sharing Personal Experiences

This is the most personal level of conversation. This is where everything is on the table and personal details are being shared. This level is typically not appropriate for a social, casual meeting. However, all of the communications skills are crucial at this stage in particular: when people are talking about matters of the heart, they require our complete attention, excellent listening skills, and skilled probing with appropriate questions.

Understanding how to converse and how to make small talk are great skills, but how do you get to that point? The answer is simple, but far from easy: you walk up, shake their hand, and say hello! If you are in the middle of a social gathering, and before the gathering, imagine the absolute worst that could happen and how likely it is, and simply relax. If you are nervous, remember that everyone is as nervous as you are. You have to focus on turning that energy into a positive force. To increase your confidence, prepare a great introduction. The best format is to say your name, your organization and position title; if appropriate, and something interesting about yourself, or something positive about the gathering.

> *Whenever you are communicating with someone, whether it is a basic conversation, a problem-solving session, or a team meeting, try to find ways in which you are alike.*

In these social gathering, it is important to act normal and do not overthink the situation. The longer you think about meeting new people, the harder it will be. Get out there, introduce yourself, and meet new people. Try to mingle as much as possible, when you get comfortable with a group of people, move on to a new group. When you hear someone's name, repeat the introduction in your head. Then, when someone new joins the group, introduce them to everyone. Finally, if you follow the conversation framework, you will have fruitful and enjoyable conversations.

4.9 Feelings & Communication

For many people, life is like a snowball. On a particularly good day, everything may go your way and make you feel like you are on top of the world. But on a bad day, unfortunate events can likewise snowball, increasing their negative effect exponentially. Successful communicators are excellent at identifying precipitating factors and adjusting their approach before the communication starts or during it. Understanding the power of precipitating factors can also help you de-personalize negative comments. This does not mean that someone having a bad day gets to dump on everyone around them; it does mean, however, that the person being dumped on can take it less personally and help the other person work through their problems.

Finding common ties can be a powerful communication tool. Think of those times when a stranger turns out not to be a stranger, that the person next to you on the train grew up in the same town that you did, or that the co-worker you never really liked enjoys woodworking as much as you do. Whenever you are communicating with someone, whether it is a basic conversation, a problem-solving session, or a team meeting, try to find ways in which you are alike. Focusing on positive connections will help you build stronger relationships and better communication.

Framing your message appropriately can greatly increase the power of your communication. Instead of starting a sentence with "you," try using the "I message" instead for feedback. This format places the responsibility with the speaker, makes a clear statement, and offers constructive feedback. Be careful not to start the sentence with some form of, "When you…" This tends to create feelings of blame and injustice.

Q1- Communication happens in three major ways:
- A- Spoken, Written, Oral
- B- Oral, Written, Formal
- C- Non-verbal, Spoken, Written
- D- Verbal, Non-verbal, Spoken

Q2- Frank asked Jess to submit the status report biweekly. Jess assumed he meant twice a week, however, Frank indicated it meant fortnightly. This is an example of:
- A- Language barrier
- B- Culture barrier
- C- Location barrier
- D- Communication error

Q3- Allison is scheduling a meeting with her offshore team. She sent an email saying the meeting will take place on Monday 10 AM. On Monday, none of her team member showed up for the meeting. What do you think went wrong?
- A- Monday was a public holiday
- B- Time zone has not been identified
- C- There is a conflict within the team
- D- Email has not been delivered

Q4-_____ is often interpreted as anxious or upset.
- A- Direct communication
- B- Emails
- C- High pitch communication
- D- Written communication

Q5- Leaning back when standing or sitting indicates a _____
- A- Casual and relaxed demeanor
- B- Stress or discomfort
- C- Stiffness and anxiety
- D- Closed mind

Q6- Gestures different significantly based on _____ and _____
- A-   Time, Day
- B-   Culture, Region
- C-   Manager, Employee
- D-   Method, Technology

Q7- While talking to an audience, you speak like a STAR, R stands for:
- A-   Revenue
- B-   Results
- C-   Role
- D-   Rule

Q8- As an active listener, you have to identify where the other person is coming from. This is called:
- A-   Frame of Reference
- B-   Active listening
- C-   Task
- D-   Results

Q9_____ mean repeating what you think the speaker said in your own words.
- A-   Communication
- B-   Paraphrasing
- C-   Rehearsal
- D-   Non-verbal

10- Using filler words such as 'uh-huh' and 'mm-hmmm' is called:
- A-   Verbal
- B-   Non-verbal
- C-   Quasi-Verbal
- D-   Oral

Answers

Q1- The correct answer is (C-Non-verbal, Spoken, Written)

Q2- The correct answer is (B-Culture barrier).

Q3- The correct answer is (B-Time zone has not been identified). It is not known whether it is 10 AM on Allison time zone or her offshore team.

Q4- The correct answer is (C-High pitch communication)

Q5- The correct answer is (A-Casual and relaxed demeanor)

Q6- The correct answer is (B-Culture, Region)

Q7- The correct answer is (B-Results)

Q8- The correct answer is (A-Frame of Reference)

Q9- The correct answer is (B-Paraphrasing)

Q10- The correct answer is (C-Quasi-Verbal)

MASTERING BODY LANGUAGE

- Defining Body Language
- Interpreting Body Language
- False Signals
- Gender Differences
- Nonverbal Communication
- Facial Expressions
- Body Language In Business
- Observing For Deception
- Develop Your Body Language
- Matching Words & Body Language

The ability to interpret body language is a skill that will enhance anyone's career. Body language is a form of communication, and it needs to be practiced like any other form of communication. Whether in sales or management, it is essential to understand the body language of others and exactly what your own body is communicating.

5.1 Defining Body Language

We are constantly communicating, even when we are not speaking. Unspoken communication makes up over half of what we tell others and they tell us. It affects our work and personal relationships. Improves negotiating, management, and interpersonal skills by correctly interpreting body language and important signals.

Understanding body language does more than improve relationships. You will get insight into the thoughts and feelings of those around you, because it is not a conscious form of communication, people betray themselves in their body language. Body language is powerful in several ways:

- **It is honest**: Body language conveys truth, even when words do not. It is honest, most of the time, as experts in body language can fake it if they intend to.
- **Creates self-awareness**: Understanding body language helps you identify your own actions that hinder success.
- **Understand feelings**: Body language shows feelings and motive such as aggression, submission, deception, etc., which will allow you to use such cues to your communication.
- **Enhance listening and communication skills**: Paying attention to body language makes someone a better listener, by hearing between the words spoken to what is being actually said.

Much of the way people communicate is nonverbal. Body language specifically focuses on physical, not tone, or pitch, and has the following characteristics.

- **Proximity**: The distance between people.
- **Positioning**: Position of a body.
- **Facial expression**: The eyes are particularly noticed.
- **Touching**: This includes objects, people, and themselves.
- **Breathing**: The rate of respiration is telling.

Our impressions of each other are based on more than words. People can have cordial conversations and not like each other. The actions that we take are stronger than our words. For example, a person may dismiss someone using body language and not saying anything negative. Like it or not, our body language makes a lasting impression on the people around us. Body language can deliver many actions including deception, confidence, nerves, boredom, emotions, attraction openness or closeness. By learning body language, you would be able to interpret such meanings and actions and use them for effective communication.

5.2 Interpreting Body Language

We are constantly reading the body language of others, even when we are not aware of it. Actively reading body language, however, will provide valuable insight and improve communication. Pay attention to the positions and movements of people around you specifically their head positions, physical gestures, and eyes. It is important to emphasize that different cultures might have different interpretations for head positions, physical gestures and eyes. Nodding head might be a sign of agreement in one culture, but a sign of disagreement in another. As an effective communicator who might communicate with clients or team members overseas, you have to be culturally sensitive and learn different interpretations in various cultures.

Open body language can come from passivity, aggression, acceptance, supplication, or relaxation.

The head is an obvious indicator of feelings and thoughts. The position of the head speaks volumes, making it the perfect place to start. While it takes practice to accurately interpret head position; the basic positions and movements are not extremely difficult to identify. Basic positions are:

- **Nodding**: Nodding typically indicates agreement. The speed of the nod, however, indicates different things. A slow nod can be a sign of interest or a polite, fake signal. Look to other eyes for confirmation. A fast nod signals impatience with the speaker.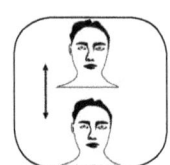

- **Head up**: This position indicates that the person is listening without bias.

- **Head down**: This position indicates disinterest or rejection for what is said. When done during an activity, it signals weakness or tiredness.

- **Tilted to the side**: This means a person is thoughtful or vulnerable. Also, it can signal trust.

- **Head high**: Holding the head high signals confidence or feelings of superiority.

- **Chin up**: The chin up indicates defiance or confidence.

- **Head forward**: Facing someone directly indicates interest. It is a positive signal.

- **Tilted down**: Tilting the head down signals disapproval.

- **Shaking**: A shaking head indicates disagreement. The faster the shaking, the stronger the disagreement.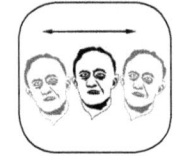

As effective communicator, you have also to translate gestures into words. Scientific studies show that the part of the human brain that comprehends words is the same part of the brain that comprehends gestures. Gestures are also called movement clusters because it is more than a body position. We use gestures when we speak, typically hand gestures, they enhance meaning, or can be used by themselves.

- **Pointing finger**: This is an aggressive movement. When a wink is added, however, it is a positive confirmation of an individual.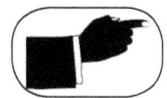

- **Finger moves side to side**: This motion acts as a warning to stop something.

- **Finger moves up and down**: This acts as a reprimand or places emphasis on what is said.

- **Thumbs up**: Thumbs up is a sign of approval.

- **Thumbs down**: This is a sign of disapproval.

- **Touch index finger to thumb**: The sign indicates an approval (OK).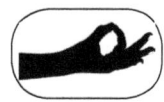

Body language is also defined as open or closed. Being open or closed has many different causes. Open body language can come from passivity, aggression, acceptance, supplication, or relaxation. Closed body language may be caused by the desire to hide, self-protection, cold, or relaxation.

Open vs. Closed Body Language	
Open	**Closed**
• **Legs not crossed**: This is an open, relaxed position.	• **Arms crossed**: This stance is often defensive or hostile.
• **Arms not crossed**: Open arms indicate openness; although the hands may indicate aggression, supplication, or insecurity, depending on their position.	• **Legs crossed when seated**: Cross legs can indicate caution. One leg over the other at the knee may indicate stubbornness.
	• **Arm or object in front of the body**: This can coincide with nervousness and is a form of self-protection.
	• **Legs crossed when standing**: This may mean someone is insecure when combined with crossed arms. By itself, it can signal interest.

Table 2 *– Open vs. Closed Body Language*

The last part of interpreting body language is interpreting eyes gestures. People give a great deal away through their eyes. The eyes are an important factor when reading a person's body language. When combined with body position, the eyes will provide a more accurate translation of body language. Typical interpretations for eyes gestures are:

- **Looking to the left**: Eyes in this direction can mean someone is remembering something. Combined with a downward look, it indicates self-communication. When looking up, it means facts are being recalled.

- **Sideways**: Looking sideways means someone is conjuring sounds. Right look is associated with imagination, and may mean a story however left look refers to accessing memory.

- **Looking to the right**: Looks to the right indicates imagination. It can mean guessing or lying. Combined with looking down, it means there is a self-question. Combined with looking up, it can mean lying.

- **Direct eye contact**: When speaking, this means sincerity and honesty. When listening, it indicates interest.

- **Wide eyes**: Widening eyes signal interest.

- **Rolled eyes**: Rolled eyes mean frustration. They can be considered a sign of hostility.

- **Blinking**: Frequent blinking indicates excitement. Infrequent blinking signals a boredom or concentration.

- **Winking**: A wink is a friendly gesture or secret joke.

- **Rubbing eyes**: Rubbing eyes may be caused by tiredness. It can also indicate disbelief or being disturbed.

5.3 False Signals

There are different factors that will create false body language signals. This is why it is so important to examine the positions and gestures as a whole when attempting to interpret body language. To prevent body language false signals, you have to become aware of these factors and think carefully when reading body language.

Posture can lead to unfair judgments and prejudices. Often, poor posture is seen as a closed body language that people assume is caused by a lack of confidence. There are, however, many different reasons why someone can have poor posture. While it is true that most people can improve on their posture, the changes that can be made to a person's musculoskeletal structure are limited. Always pay attention to other cues, and do not make rash judgments based solely on posture. Some causes of poor posture are:

- **Injury**: Both acute injuries and repetitive motion injuries can alter someone's posture.
- **Illness**: Autoimmune diseases, such as arthritis, can damage the skeletal structure.
- **Skeletal structure**: Scoliosis and other problems with the spine will affect posture.
- **Temperature**: People may take a closed posture when they are cold.

> *Closed body language may be caused by the desire to hide, self-protection, cold, or relaxation.*

Another aspect that might send false signals for body language is personal space. Personal space is the actual distance between you and the other person with whom you are communicating. Invading personal space might cause false body language. Invading personal space is seen as an act of hostility, however, there are reasons why people will invade personal space that have nothing to do with hostility such culture, background or activity type. Each culture has different boundaries and personal space. Also, personal history and background will affect an individual's concept of personal space. And finally, some activities require people to work closely. This should be considered before assuming someone is invading personal space.

Western societies typically use five different zones, depending on the social situations. These are:

1. **12 feet**: This zone is for the public. The purpose is to avoid physical interaction.
2. **4 feet**: This zone is reserved for social interactions such as business settings. Touching requires the individual to move forward.
3. **18 inches**: This is a personal zone. It allows contact, and it is reserved for friends and family.
4. **6 inches**: This zone is reserved for close relationships. This zone can be invaded in crowds or sports.
5. **0 to 6 inches**: This zone is reserved for intimate relationships.

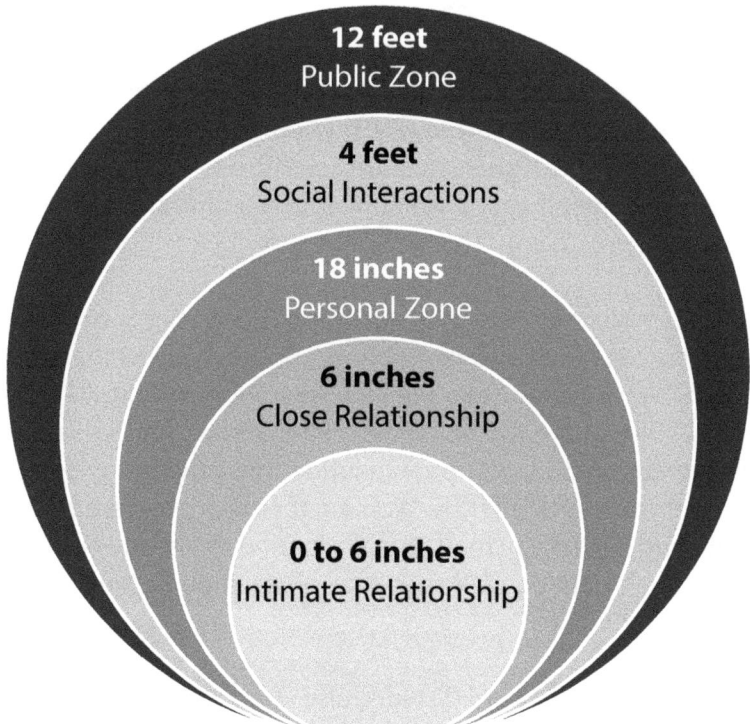

Figure 7 – *Five Different Zones Of Personal Space*

Quick movements may be interpreted as a sign of nervousness. They may, however, be used to draw attention to specific information when speaking. Consistent jerking movements, however, do not always indicate nerves or negative emotions. Do not make a snap judgment about quick movements. There are reasons why movements may seem quick or jerking such as stress, illness, exhaustion or cold. You have to understand the impacts of such quick movements on the body language.

Another reason that might lead to false body language is fidgeting. Most people fidget from time to time. In interviews and social settings, fidgeting can indicate nervousness, boredom, frustration, stress, or self-consciousness. It is an outlet to release feelings or an attempt at self-comfort. Besides emotions, there are a number of other reasons why people may fidget such as hormone or blood sugar imbalances, imbalanced brain chemistry, or medications.

5.4 Gender Differences

Not all body language is universal. There are differences in the way that men and women communicate. Body language is often confused between genders. In order to prevent miscommunications, it is important to understand the signals that are common to most people as well as the different signals that men and women communicate with their body language.

Men and women share the universal facial expressions, but there are some differences in use and perception. For example, women typically tend to smile more often than men. Women frequently smile to be polite or fulfill cultural expectations. The meanings behind smiles are often misinterpreted. Additionally, people judge the same facial expressions on men and women differently. Women, for example, were thought to be angrier and less happy than men, according to a study published by the American Psychological Association, even though they all had the same facial expressions.

Personal space and personal distance also change with each individual. Everyone has his or her own idea of personal distance, which is the comfortable distance that someone wishes to keep from another person.

Gender, however, often affects one's sense of personal distance. Men generally take more space than women, and they employ larger personal distances. Men are less likely to stand close to each other, even when they are all friends. Additionally, they create larger buffer zones using items such as coats, cups, papers, etc. Men usually expect their buffer zones to be respected and do not respond well to someone invading their personal space.

On the other side, women generally employ smaller personal distances with each other or with male friends. They tend to increase personal distance with strange men. Women also create buffer zones, but they are typically smaller than male buffer zones. Women are more likely to draw back when their zones are invaded, and female buffer zones are not always respected. People are more likely to move a woman's purse than a man's coat.

There are some subtle differences to note when interpreting female body language. Culture plays a role in what is considered appropriate body language. Female body language changes over time, and it is not universal to all women. There are, however, some basic actions that many women have in common. The same applies to male. Male body language is not universal to all men. There are, however, certain aspects of body language that are common to many men, however, male body language is often seen as more aggressive and dominating. Women are sometimes encouraged to adapt male body language in the workplace.

Body language differences between men and women	
Men	**Women**
• **Stance**: Men often choose wide stances to increase their size. Spread legs with a straight back, both sitting and standing, indicates confidence. Closed body language does not. • **Eye contact**: Men will make eye contact, but eye contact can be seen as a dominating or hostile act when it lasts too long. Occasional eye aversion is normal. Like women, pupils dilate with interest. • **Mirroring**: Men do not typically mirror each other. They often mirror women to show their interest. • **Legs and feet**: Like women, the legs and feet typically point in the direction of a man's interest. This includes romantic interest. • **Smiling**: Men do not smile as often as women in social settings; their facial expressions are often reserved. They do, however, occasionally use forced smiles. Men often smile when happy or to engage someone's interest. • **Hands**: Men are more likely to fidget than women. This is not necessarily a sign of insecurity or boredom, just a way to use energy.	• **Body Position and posture**: Many women use closed body language. This may stem from a cultural convention to appear smaller. Women, however, will straighten their posture to look more attractive. • **Leaning**: Women will lean forward when they are interested in something or someone. They lean away when displeased or uncomfortable. • **Smiling**: We have already mentioned that women are more likely to smile. While it is often a friendly gesture, it is a probably a polite gesture when the eyes are not engaged. • **Eye contact**: Eye contact indicates interest either in what is said or the individual. Dilated pupils are another sign of interest. • **Mirroring**: Women often mirror, or copy, the actions of each other. They will occasionally mirror men. • **Legs and feet**: The legs and feet typically point in the direction of a woman's interest. This includes romantic interest. • **Touching**: Women are more likely to touch each other than men are. • **Tapping**: Tapping or fidgeting is a sign that a woman is annoyed or uncomfortable.

Table 3 *– Body Language Differences Between Men And Women*

5.5 Nonverbal Communication

We all communicate nonverbally. The image that we project from our nonverbal communication affects the way that our spoken communication is received. While interpreting body language is important, it is equally important to understand what your nonverbal communication is telling others. It takes more than words to persuade others. Many gestures that we make are unconscious movements or mannerisms. Being aware of what our gestures mean will make us aware of what we are communicating. Some of the unconscious gestures are:

- **Biting nails**: This may mean insecurity or nerves.
- **Turning away**: Looking away indicates that you do not believe someone.
- **Pulling ears**: Tugging at ears can indicate indecision.
- **Head tilt**: A brief head tilt means interest. Holding a tilt equals boredom.
- **Open palms**: Showing palms is a sign of innocence or sincerity.
- **Rubbing hands together**: Rubbing hands together is a sign of excitement or anticipation.
- **Touching the chin**: This signals that a decision is being made.
- **Hand on the cheek**: Touching the cheek indicates someone is thinking.
- **Drumming fingers**: This is a sign of impatience.
- **Touching the nose**: People often associate touching the nose with lying. It can also signal doubt or rejection.

You are always sending signals to other people. These signals come through body language, voice, appearance, and personal distance. Body language includes posture, gestures, and facial expressions. A person's hygiene and dress send signals to others and people make negative assumptions based on a disheveled appearance. Also, too great a personal distance makes people appear cold. On the other hand, not respecting the personal distance of others will have negative consequences. Finally is the voice and tone, which is important to the way we communicate as emotions are conveyed through tone.

Miscommunication is a common problem in personal and business relationships. Paying attention to the way that you communicate will help prevent any miscommunications. You must take note of the tone, pitch, and timbre of your voice. People tend to naturally respect deeper voices. High-pitched voices are viewed as a sign of immaturity. Even a neutral tone can make a person appear weak or insecure when there is a higher pitch at the end of a statement, like questions have.

When speaking, keep a moderate pace. Speaking too quickly will cause confusion, and speaking too slowing will make it difficult to keep attention. Speak up; quiet voices can be viewed as submissive and be careful, however, not accidentally yell. Finally, tone conveys emotion, so avoid sarcasm and condescension. Vary your tone to prevent boring listeners with a monotone presentation.

Posture is the basis of body language communication. People respond well to good posture, and having good posture improves physical and emotional health. Slouching is seen as a sign of insecurity or weakness. Confident body language demands good posture. Standing straight communicates confidence. It will also prevent musculoskeletal pain. However, hunching over is closed body language and can signal unhappiness or insecurity. Ducking or shrugging the head is a protective or submissive move to appear smaller. It is not equated with confidence.

To project the right posture, stand and sit straight. Straight posture maintains the natural curve of the spine. This is achieved by pulling in the abdominal muscles, pushing the shoulders back, and lifting the chest. Hold the head upright and look to the front. This will protect the natural shape of the neck. And finally, relax. Your posture should not be forced or stiff, someone with straight posture should look and feel relaxed.

5.6 Facial Expressions

Facial expressions are an important part of body language. We use our faces to express ourselves, and we all interpret the facial expressions we see. While some facial expressions are cultural, some facial expressions are universal. Understanding the basics of facial expressions and decoding them will help you determine what people are feeling and facilitate better communication.

Many scientists agree that facial expressions are linked to emotions. Different feelings create physical responses within the body, and facial expressions are emotional responses to situations. Because of the emotional connection, it is not easy to continually fake facial expressions. A flash of true emotion will typically flicker across the face, even when feelings are kept in check. Not only are emotions shown with facial expressions; the degree of emotion a person feels is visible on the face. For example, you can see the difference between a face that shows sadness and one that shows sorrow.

We all hide negative or unwanted emotions from time to time. We can even mask our facial expressions to fit social situations. Feelings can occasionally slip out in the form of micro-expressions. These brief, involuntary expressions betray emotions, and they typically last 1/25 of a second. For example, someone gives a brief sneer but smiles when running into an acquaintance. Most people do not consciously notice micro-expressions. In fact, roughly ten percent of people will knowingly pick up on the micro-expressions of others.

Most micro-expressions are based on universal facial expressions. Being aware of these facial expressions will make micro expressions easier to catch. Noticing micro-expressions can help determine if someone is lying. It is not foolproof, however. For example, someone can be afraid of being caught in a lie or of not being believed.

When analyzing micro-expressions, the FACS becomes helpful. The Facial Action Coding System (FACS) is a complex system attributed to Dr. Paul Ekman. This system breaks down the muscle movements of micro-expressions into numbered action units (AUs). The muscles that relax or contract with emotion are identified to show the feeling behind each movement of the face. There are AUs identified in the upper and lower face. The meanings behind these involuntary muscle movements are interpreted by the FACS system. The intensity, duration, and asymmetry of expressions are also noted.

Many facial expressions are learned from one's family and culture. There are, however, facial expressions that all people are believed to share in common. These are the universal facial expressions. Success with FACS and interpreting micro-expressions requires an understanding of universal facial expressions. There are different lists of universal facial expressions, but most lists include the same six facial expressions.

- **Happiness**: More than a smile is needed to indicate happiness. Genuine happiness should include the eyes. Eyelids crinkle a crow's feet become visible.
- **Anger**: A frown typically accompanies anger. Additionally, the eyes narrow, the chin points forward, and the eyebrows furrow.
- **Fear**: Wide eyes and slightly raised eyebrows signal fear. The lips may be parted or stretched when the mouth is closed.
- **Surprise**: Surprise is similar to fear. The eyebrows fully raise and the eyes are wide with surprise. The mouth, however, is usually open.
- **Sadness**: The mouth turns down when someone is sad. A crease in the forehead and quivering chin accompany this slight frown.
- **Disgust**: The expression of disgust includes the nose. The nose wrinkles, the lips part, and the eyes narrow.

5.7 Body Language In Business

Body language can provide people in business with a key advantage. Learn how to adjust your body language to each situation, as you identify the needs, thoughts, and feelings of those you do business with every day. A basic understanding of body language will strengthen negotiating strategies and other business tactics.

Powerful communication breeds confidence and respect. It is important that people sense power without aggression. Communicating with power requires practice, but it is an effective business tool. There are several powerful movements such as:

- **Stance**: A wide stance with the feet apart indicates power. Hands on the hips with the elbows out take up more space and also indicates power.

- **Positioning**: Avoid open space at your back. It is known to elevate stress. Open spaces can be used to make others more vulnerable.
- **Walk**: Walk quickly and take long strides. Be careful not to run, and keep the back and neck erect.
- **Handshake**: Offer a firm handshake, and keep the hand vertical. Placing the palm up because it is a submissive gesture. The palm down is a dominating gesture.
- **Sitting**: Sit with the legs slightly apart. Another powerful pose is sitting with one leg crossed over the other and hands behind the head. Be careful, however, because this position makes many women uncomfortable.

International business means working with different cultural backgrounds. While certain expressions are universally recognized, many gestures are cultural. It is essential to research the etiquette and communication style of any culture you do business with ahead of time. Monitor body language to build trust with business partners. You should remain relaxed, smile genuinely and actively listen would all help build trust with business partners.

Another key body language aspect to consider while conducting business is mirroring. Mirroring helps build rapport and occurs when we copy the movements and gestures of others to show similarities. The perception that people are similar creates trust. Typically mirroring comes easier to women and women will mirror each other in social settings. Men usually mirror women in romantic situations. In the business setting, consciously mirroring a client or colleague will have dramatic results. You can mirror a smile if your client does smile or copy their gestures or monitor their speech tone and pitch. All these mirroring, while done carefully, will send signs of trust and rapport.

5.8 Observing For Deception

Body language can expose deception. Close observation of body language can indicate that someone is hiding something. Be careful about interpreting every action as a lie. A number of factors, including stress and insecurity will cause suspicious body language. When there are multiple indications of deception in a person's body language, however, further investigation may be warranted. We all communicate with our hands. We can even communicate deception without knowing what we are doing. Several movements can indicate someone is hiding something such as:

- **Palms down**: Showing your palms is a sign of sincerity. Keeping the palms down signals that someone is hiding something.

- **Self-touching**: Self-touching may be a calming action, but be alert when someone touches this or her face. Hands at the nose and mouth are often seen as an attempt to hide the spoken lie.

- **Hidden hands**: Hand gestures are a natural part of communication. Many people will suddenly hide their hands when telling lies. Lack of hand movement may also indicate lying.

We have already mentioned smiling. A forced smile does not reach the eyes. Alone, a forced smile can simply indicate that someone is trying to be polite. Always pay close attention when other deceptive movement clusters accompany a forced smile, as they can add additional proof that a person could be lying such as:

- **Tight smiles**: A tight, thin-lipped smile can indicate that someone is concealing information.

- **Closed mouth**: Genuine smiles are typically open. A closed smile, however, could be an effort to hide bad teeth.

- **Licking lips**: Lying can cause the mouth to dry out. People who lie are more likely to lick their lips after speaking.

Also, deception can be identified by observing eyes. The eyes are called the windows to the soul. The eyes continually communicate feelings. A person's eye contact can betray that he or she is being deceptive. Some of the gestures are:

- **Little to no eye contact**: A complete lack of eye contact may be an indication that someone is nervous and being deceptive, but it is not always an indication of lying. There could be cultural reasons for this behavior, so always be aware of any outside factors.

- **Looking to the left**: Moving the gaze to the left may indicate deception. It signals the imagination is being engaged. Left-handed individuals will shift their eyes to the right.

- **Unmoving eyes**: Some people who lie can look directly ahead without moving their eyes. They will not always shift their gaze or look away.

Posture can easily signal when a person is being deceptive. Lying will cause someone to focus more on his or her body language. This can cause people to exercise too much control or shift posture. Some of the postures are:

- **Being still**: People who try to control their movements may be very still. Slight changes in positioning are normal. Abnormally still individuals may be hiding something.

- **Extreme changes**: Deception causes anxiety in most people. When body language changes from defensive positions to open, friendly postures. The clumsier these transitions increase the likelihood of deception.

- **Voice and movements do not correspond**: Body language typically reflects the voice and message of a speaker. When this is not the case, lying is indicated. For example, someone uses closed, defensive body language with a friendly tone and interaction.

5.9 Develop Your Body Language

People make snap judgments about each other based on body language. It is possible to improve your body language and the way that others view you. Give an air of confidence when meeting with colleagues and potential clients. Understanding the subtleties of body language makes it easier to improve your own. Simply pay attention to what you say and do.

It is important to be aware of your movements and what they mean. The best way to do this, however, is to make sure that the movements are genuine. Faked body language typically looks disjointed and unnatural and people can subconsciously pick up on these movements.

Look and act natural by:
- *Relaxing: Try to relax and implement open body language. This will help prevent any nervous body signals.*
- *Watching your hands: Use comfortable gestures when talking. Do not hide your hands, and try to avoid fidgeting or touching your face.*
- *Maintaining eye contact: Maintain eye contact, but do stare at people.*
- *Smiling: Avoid fake smiles and give genuine smiles to instill trust.*
- *Watching your head: Look ahead; tilting is submissive. Nod occasionally to signal your interest.*

Improve body language by increasing personal confidence. Everyone has a personal level of confidence that is evident in body language. There are simple ways that can help improve confidence and body language. Our appearance affects our confidence and dressing well will help improve our self-esteem. Also, an open posture will induce confidence and it will also improve the way others see you. Speak in a confident tone to increase your feelings of confidence and do not mumble. Straight posture automatically increases confidence and alertness. Avoid slouching, but remain relaxed. And finally, maintain open body positions. Open body positions communicate a relaxed and confident demeanor while closed body positions indicate defensiveness.

Practice is the key to improve your body language and eventually to success. Many people have poor body mechanics. They do not realize the mechanics to alter their posture or positions. Practicing body language in front of a mirror will give an accurate evaluation of what you are communicating. Just observe how you stand, observe your gesture, breathing, hands movement, head movement, and your tone. You might also which to video record yourself while talking and then watch and study the recording to identify areas of improvements.

5.10 Matching Words & Body Language

The key to instilling trust is matching body language to the words spoken. Movements will confirm or contradict what is said. Gestures will easily match what is said if the words reflect genuine feeling. Emotional awareness is necessary to communicate exactly what you mean. Unresolved emotions can affect body language.

We do not control our involuntary movements. Emotions can affect our breathing, posture, gestures, and micro-expressions. People subconsciously pick up on involuntary movements, particularly when they contradict what is said. For example, increased respiration can indicate stress or anxiety. When practicing body language, be aware of involuntary movements. Reducing stress and finding healthy ways to express emotion will help limit involuntary movements.

Communication is much more effective when you say what you mean. Deception is often part of polite communication. This will affect body language and movement, however, you should always practice being respectful and honest in your speech, and be always consistent. The key is to be consistently honest and open when communicating with others.

To judge you, people pay more attention to actions than words. We typically make decisions about someone within four seconds of a meeting. This is largely based on body language and behavior. If your body language is hostile, it does not matter how kind your words or tone are. Be aware of what your actions and gestures are communicating to those around you. Practice your body language skills and decode the body language of others.

Chapter 5 – Mastering Body Language

Q1- Unspoken communication makes up over _____ of what we tell others and they tell us.
- A- Third
- B- Fourth
- C- Half
- D- 90%

Q2- Much of the way people communicate is _____
- A- Oral
- B- Verbal
- C- Written
- D- Non-verbal

Q3- Leslie is a project manager in charge for Delta product. The product is being developed with teams from Canada, USA, India and Ukraine. Beyond the product specifications, Leslie needs to pay attention to:
- A- Product Design
- B- Cultural Diversity
- C- Technology for communication
- D- Team leaders' responsibilities

Q4- During a video conference call with his team in India and USA, Mike asked both Anil and Matt on whether they agree about the suggested task durations. Both of Anil and Matt nod their heads. Mike was happy and moved forward. Later, tasks were slipping behind schedule. What was a one important thing Mike ignored?
- A- Task dependency
- B- Confirming with Anil and Matt verbally
- C- Maintaining daily checkup with Anil and Matt
- D- Sharing a minutes of meeting report

Q5- A chin up gesture refers to:
- A- A person who is listening without bias
- B- A person who is defiant or confident
- C- A person who disapproves
- D- A person who is listening with bias

Q6- A slow nod is different and carries different meaning than a quick nod. A quick node refers to _____while slow node refers to _____
- A- Agreement or impatience, polite or fake signal
- B- Fake signal, Agreement
- C- Weakness, Strength
- D- Anger, Happiness

Q7- To show that you are interested about the trainer suggestion, your head should:
- A- Lean backward
- B- Lean forward
- C- Titled down
- D- Shaking

Q8- An indication that the discussion lacks interest, the body language gesture could be closed such as:
- A- Arms not crossed
- B- Legs crossed when standing
- C- Head is up
- D- Thumbs is up

Q9- Maintaining personal space is important while communicating with others. The zone that is reserved for social interactions such as business meetings is:
- A- 12 feet
- B- 4 feet
- C- 18 inches
- D- 6 inches

Q10- How is eye contact different between men and women?
- A- Eye contact for men is perceived to be dominating or hostile when it takes too long. For women, it is a sign of interest.
- B- Eye contact for women is a sign of hostility, while for men it is a sign of interest.
- C- Eye contact for men and women is the same
- D- Usually, women stare more often than men

Q11-During the weekly status update meeting, Katy, the project manager checks on Milos tasks, and while she inquiries about his progress, Milos responded, while touching his nose, that the task is on track. What is Katy supposed to do next?
- A- Katy needs to move ahead and check on other teams' reports
- B- Katy must ask for an evidence from Milos
- C- Milos needs to consider Katy's body language
- D- Katy is supposed to update her plans accordingly

Q12- A palm down gesture is _____
- A- A submissive gesture
- B- A dominating gesture
- C- A relaxing gesture
- D- A closed gesture

Q13- While meeting with clients for the first time, James make sure he mirrors his counterpart, as mirroring conveys:
- A- Trust and rapport
- B- Happiness and excitement
- C- Anger and frustration
- D- Lack of seriousness

Q14- In a business meeting, to look and act natural, it is important that you:
- A- Relax and watch your hands
- B- Smile continuously
- C- Remain silent and never talk
- D- Avoid eye contact

Q15- To instill trust, your smile must be:
- A- Continuous
- B- Incongruous
- C- Genuine
- D- Submissive

Answers

Q1- The correct answer is (C-Half).

Q2- The correct answer is (D-Non-verbal).

Q3- The correct answer is (B-Cultural Diversity) and differences between various team members in these countries.

Q4- The correct answer is (B-Confirming with Anil and Matt verbally) as nodding their heads might have different interpretations. Mike should have immediately confirmed his understanding and their agreement about the task durations. Then, he could have shared minutes of meeting, and followed up with daily checkups if required.

Q5- The correct answer is (B-A person who is defiant or confident).

Q6- The correct answer is (A-Agreement or impatience, polite or fake signal)

Q7- The correct answer is (B-Learn forward) as a sign of interest.

Q8- The correct answer is (B-Legs crossed when standing).

Q9- The correct answer is (B-4 feet)

Q10- The correct answer is (A-Eye contact for men is perceived to be dominating or hostile when it takes too long. For women, it is a sign of interest)

Q11- The correct answer is (B-Katy must ask for an evidence from Milos) as touching his nose could be interpreted as a sign of doubt or lying. Katy needs evidence before adjusting her plan or moving forward.

Q12- The correct answer is (B-A dominating gesture).

Q13- The correct answer is (A-Trust and rapport).

Q14- The correct answer is (A-Relax and watch your hands).

Q15- The correct answer is (C-Genuine).

EFFECTIVE PRESENTATION SKILLS

- Creating The Plan
- Deliver Your Presentation
- Using Flip Charts
- Impress With PowerPoint
- Using Whiteboards
- Using Videos And Audio
- EIEI Model
- Present Like Steve Jobs

In today's workplaces, you have regularly to present a business report to your manager, a business case to the company board or a proposal to your team. As a leader, a manager, a trainer, a meeting facilitator, speaker, or seminar discussion leader, you have to master presentation skills to ensure your message is delivered completely, concisely and successfully to your audience. Mastering presentation skills requires preparation, planning and dedication for improvement. Creating and delivering presentations that would wow your audience cannot happen over night. As a leader or manager, you have to learn the skills, acquire and practice them to become a true proficient in delivering outstanding presentations.

6.1 Creating The Plan

We will look at the beginning steps to follow when creating a plan to improve your presentation kills. The first thing to look at is to perform a needs analysis. This will help you to understand your audience and provide you with the answers to a few basic questions. A basic outline and some minor research would then be utilized to help create the basic program that will assist you in developing greater Presentation Skills. A needs analysis measures what skills the audience has and what they need from the presentation. It indicates how to deliver the right presentation at the right time with the right content to the right audience. You need important questions such as:

- Who is the audience?
- What do they actually know about the subject?
- What do they expect to know new from the presentation?
- What is their level of education?
- Which departments or companies do they represent?

Once you find answers to these questions, you will be able to create an outline for your presentation before even writing a single world. To develop the outline, group the topics that fit together logically, and create headings that reflect these topics. Add headings for an introduction and presentation objectives at the beginning and a wrap-up and evaluation at the end, and your basic outline is complete.

The needs analysis has likely produced much of the supporting content required to build the plan. However, if information gaps exist, return to your audience or subject matter experts and ask questions. If you are using a word processor, create a template so your material is consistent from the beginning. Assign a preliminary time length to each topic based on the total time available for the presentation. When writing, aim for brevity. The more you say, the less the audience remembers.

Make sure to validate your finalized content before you move on to editing. As you edit, write for the ear, not for the eyes. Make sure sentences are twenty words or less and only convey one thought. Use simple, familiar words and make sure that you have provided the definitions of any terms important to the learning experience.

6.2 Deliver Your Presentation

Now it is time to determine what methods you will use to deliver your presentation. Are you going to lecture or have a discussion? If you must lecture occasionally, use strategies to make the delivery more interactive such as engaging the audience, asking questions and using role-playing. Instead, you might decide to break the audience into small groups, dyads or triads to manage, control and enhance the discussions.

A small group experience provides direction toward specific learning goals, and provides a high degree of participant involvement, while using pairs, dyads, groups of 2 persons, provides unlimited options for simple interactive experiences. You can say, "Turn to the person on your right and…" Using dyads manages the attention span, the extent of influence, and the focus of the goal; hence, the learning experience is relatively intimate. Finally, trios, groups of 3 persons, expand the focus and experience opportunities. A measure of intimacy is still retained, but multiple viewpoints can be contributed. Triads are useful for producing definitions, establishing priorities, or providing an on-going support system.

Other ways to present and facilitate learning experiences includes role-playing. Role-playing allows participants to act out a behavioral role. This exercise done with small groups or the large group allows members to expand their awareness of varying points of view, and provides an experiential learning opportunity. A role-play can be used in several ways; to solve a participant problem, clarify or sharpen an issue, or demonstrate a skill approach to a task. Importantly, it gives people an opportunity to practice a skill or approach in a safe environment and use the experience later on the job.

Here are several tips for managing role play exercises:
- *Obtain volunteers, rather than making assignments*
- *Use role play later in the training session, when participants know each other better*
- *Select low-threat situations, such as a work group holding a staff meeting.*

Problem solving experiences are increasingly popular in presentations, primarily training, because they allow participants to gain real world experience that often provides direct transfer back to the job. If you wish to structure your presentation in problem solving setting, you must proceed in structured manner. First, your presentation must define the problem and generate data about it. Then, the audience will work to generate potential solutions and subsequently, vote and select a solution with an implementation plan. A training presentation may use any combination of delivery methods as long as the net result is to achieve learning outcomes and consider organizational requirements and constraints.

Advanced Methods To Use In Presentations		
Phase	**Method**	**Description**
Defining the problem and generating data about it	Pareto Analysis	Vilfredo Pareto, a mathematician and economist coined the "80/20" rule. A Pareto Analysis allows you to group and analyze data for a problem and focus on 20% of causes that generate 80% of problems.
	Force Field Analysis	Kurt Lewin defined driving forces and restraining forces that influence the solution to a problem.
Generating potential solutions	Brainstorming	Brainstorming allows a group to generate a large volume of ideas about a problem, or potential solutions. Later, the results must be condensed to a workable number of ideas, typically through grouping, and then voted on.
	The Delphi Technique	Originally used by the RAND corporation, the Delphi technique allows the anonymous generating of ideas which are then filtered.
Selecting and implementing a solution	Ranking	Participants rank options on a given scale, with or without criteria.
	The Journalist's Six Questions	Use "who, what, when, where, why and how" questions to generate data.

Table 4 – *Advanced Methods To Use In Presentations*

6.3 Using Flip Charts

Information written on flip charts enhances the learning process. During a presentation, the use of flip charts serves to inform participants, record information, and focus attention on a topic. They represent a simple, low-cost learning aid with no requirements for power or technology, and no worries about burned-out bulbs or darkened rooms. Flip charts add versatility to a presentation, and allow the presenter to use creativity to enhance the learning process.

The best colors to use on your flip charts are blue, black, and green which offer the greatest visibility, and blue is the most pleasing color. Avoid purple, brown, pink, and yellow for any type of general printing.

At a minimum, you will need a flip chart easel, several pads of flip chart paper, a few sets of colored markers, and masking tape for posting the results of exercises. Also handy are several packages of sticky notes to flag specific pages, and a straight edge. You may want to plan to cover up information that you will reveal at a given time during the presentation and then have some pre-cut paper available, sized appropriately for the text.

If you are bringing pre-written charts to an off-site presentation, you will also need some type of container to protect the pages. There are many good reasons to pre-write your flip chart content.

- **Confidence**: You are in control of the material for your presentation such as design, organization, and appearance, which also helps reduce nervousness.
- **Appearance**: Your material has a specific "look and feel" that is not necessarily easy to achieve when prepared during a session.
- **Time**: With your charts ready ahead of the presentation, the time during a presentation is used for learning activities, not writing, which keeps your back to the participants.

Good use of color can make the difference in the dynamics of a presentation and participants acceptance of the content. Conversely, the effect of a great chart can suffer from the poor use of color. According to the Optical Society of America, blue, black, and green offer the greatest visibility, and blue is the most pleasing color. Avoid purple, brown, pink, and yellow for any type of general printing.

Also, the use of two or three color combinations can be very effective. Red and orange should only be used as accent colors for bullets, underlines, or arrows, or for key words when everything else is in black or blue and, always avoid orange and blue together while you should never use yellow. Eventually, when creating your charts, take some time to think about the colors you are using, and how they can enhance the understanding of your topic.

Nothing goes as planned, hence, you have always to have a backup plan or plan B. Paper is not permanent, even if you are presenting at your own location. And if you are flying with your materials or shipping them, packages do occasionally get lost or damaged. You will need a backup plan in case something happens. Below are some tasks for creating your Plan B:

- Keep documents on your computer organized by event or course, reflecting the content and order sequence of each flip chart.
- Make paper handouts of the most critical information on the charts.
- Take pictures of the chart pages, and have the camera or images with you on site.
- If you have time to re-create some of your charts, enlist a volunteer to help you reconstruct the most critical ones.
- If you will be returning to the site, consider leaving a set of your charts with a trusted colleague until you return.
- As time permits, duplicate your charts in PowerPoint. Although you will probably continue to use flip charts, having them available in PowerPoint becomes a backup.

6.4 Impress With PowerPoint

Microsoft PowerPoint is a commanding tool for creating visual screens for a presentation. Visuals created in PowerPoint and projected on a screen are often easier to see in a large room than information displayed on a flip chart. Using PowerPoint allows you to add emphasis to important concepts and helping to increase retention of information, it adds variety to your presentation and makes it easier to display images, charts, or graphs possibly too complex for a flip chart. Also, PowerPoint files can easily be shared with participants or others after the session.

How to create a great PowerPoint presentation?	
• Display only one major concept on each slide • Use short phrases or bullet points rather than paragraphs • Limit each line of text to no more than 7-8 words • Allow only 7-8 lines of text per slide, if not less. • Use images sparingly; one or two per slide. • Leave a good amount of blank space in your presentation. • Create a title for each slide. • Create a number for each slide. • Use effects, transitions animation, and sound very sparingly. • Avoid cluttering your slides. • Use simple sans serif fonts such as Helvetica or Arial for readability • Select a point size of 32 or larger for titles, and 20 points for body text	• Use colors that work well together, such as yellow or white on a dark blue background. • Check the readability and visibility of your fonts and color choices with the lighting in the room in which you will present. • Make sure to match your slides to the purpose of the presentation • Develop a template and stick to it for a consistent look and feel • Check your equipment, computer settings, and room lighting in advance • Before your presentation, turn off screensavers, instant messaging, and email notifications • Make sure that your computer's power management console will not automatically shut the system down after a set amount of time.

Table 5 – *How To Create A Great PowerPoint Presentation?*

As with flip charts, nothing goes as planned, and a backup plan must be in place. While technology allows you to make great enhancements to a presentation, it also offers more opportunities for technical trouble. Always, make one or more backup copies of your PowerPoint file on the computer on which you plan to show the presentation. Additionally, copy your PowerPoint file onto a USB Drive. That way, if you have a computer problem, you can move the file to another one, if available. It is also advised to bring sufficient printed copies of your presentation for participants in case of major technical failures. If all else fails, be ready to write your key points on a flip chart.

6.5 Using Whiteboards

A whiteboard is the name for any glossy-surfaced writing board where non-permanent markings can be made. Unlike the predecessor chalk-board, there is no chalk dust, and markings remain longer than they would on a chalkboard. Whiteboards have been around since the 1970's, and are now vastly improved and more affordable compared to early models. The use of a whiteboard helps to promote interactivity during a presentation.

Traditional whiteboards are attached to the wall or are available in free-standing frames. Unlike pre-written flip chart paper sheets, whiteboards cannot easily be moved from site to site. However, they are usually lar-ger, and are useful for recording the results of small group exercises or spontaneous information arising in a discussion. A traditional white-board requires a set of wet or dry erase whiteboard markers, a white-board eraser, and whiteboard cleaning solution.

In recent years, new type of whiteboards had evolved. An electronic whiteboard looks like a traditional whiteboard, but is a unique combin-ation of hardware and software. The surface is connected to a computer and a projector. A projector beams the computer's desktop onto the board's surface, where users control the computer using a pen, finger, or other device. Because the markings on the whiteboard are digitized, the resulting electronic information can be stored, printed, or shared in real time with participants in other locations.

When using a traditional whiteboard, you should have extra markers on hand, because they tend to dry up easily. If your presentation is longer than one day, plan to make a backup of your work from the computer to a USB flash drive in the event that they are erased overnight. Instead, if you are working with an electronic whiteboard and encounter tech-nical issues, you can show a previously created PowerPoint presentation through a projector. Plan to carry at least one copy of the PowerPoint handouts for duplication if needed. You can always quickly jot down key points on a flip chart. Regardless of which type of whiteboard is used, key content should be available in a handout master or on flip chart pages as a backup.

6.6 Using Videos And Audio

Audio and video are very much part of our everyday lives, so they are accepted and even expected media in a presentation. They are attractive options for a presentation because they provide learners with more dimensions by which to receive information. While video and audio both represent a one-way communication to participants, the opportunity to use them as part of learning exercises or in the ensuing discussions adds value to the presentation.

Audio can be used as a standalone option, as part of the video, or even created by the participants, such as an exercise to write and sign a song. For video with audio you will need some type of player, depending upon the media type. You will also need a projector and a projection screen and speakers or sound system.

Audio and video can be used to enrich a presentation or training session by showing an interview with a subject matter expect, a demo of a product or small movie clip to deliver a specific message. In all cases, you have to preselect and qualify all your audio and video clips before your presentation. You need to ensure they are appropriate and relevant to the presentation subject and audience. If you would be browsing the audio and video files from the Internet, just ensure you have a local copy; if copyright laws permit, in your local PC or computer to avoid any technical problems during the presentation.

 Use the EIEI Model to create outstanding presentations. EIEI stands for: Excite, Inform, Engage and Inspire.

Regardless of the method you use for your audio and video, it is essential to have a backup plan in the event that something goes awry with the technology. Have one or two backup copies of your media, perhaps on a USB flash drive and a DVD. You must also test everything before the presentation by playing the audio and video files in your computer as well as in the presentation venue. Additionally, create a handout with the key concepts contained in your video and possibly capturing screen shots directly from the video, if permissible by copyright and add them to a PowerPoint file. If, for any reason, none is feasible, consider substituting a role-play between you and the selected participants. Above all, today's participants understand the gotchas when technology is involved, and will probably be empathetic as you carry on your presentation as if it was no big deal.

6.7 EIEI Model

Now you have all preparations for your presentation ready, it is the time to think how you actually want to deliver it. All these preparations are worthless if you cannot as a person presents, speaks, communicates and engages your audience perfectly. This is why public speaking skills are very vital to deliver outstanding presentations. To deliver outstanding presentations, you can trust our EIEI model. EIEI model stands for four-step process, which can smoothly bring the audience to your side and make them, not only prepared, but also excited to join your presentation. EIEI model four steps are:

1. **Excite**: As a presenter, your audience wants to be excited. You need to bring something new, something awesome, and something exciting to the presentation. These could be new facts, or new skills they will acquire during the course of the presentation. There is always something exciting that should have brought those people to your presentation, find it, and use it.

2. **Inform**: Now your audience are excited to learn the new technology, skills or new information, It is the time now to till them how you will deliver it to them, what is the outline of the presentation, the major outcome, how long it will take…etc. Your audience should know after this step what you expect from them and what they expect from you.

3. **Engage**: During the presentation, your audience expects to be part of it not out of it. Most presentations are two-way communication; therefore, you have to keep engaging your audience by asking questions, conducting role-plays, playing group games…etc. Your audience must be lively engaged in your presentation, they must feel dynamic and the course or presentation is interactive. Otherwise, boredom will haunt everyone of them.

4. **Inspire**: This is the step where you deliver your key messages or key concepts and make them through the audience. You have to inspire them that they can learn the new skill, or can apply the new technique, that they will be different people after the course of presentation or training as they acquired something new.

As a presenter, if you follow the **EIEI** model consistently, in all of your presentations, whether these are training courses, products demonstrations, or team presentations, you will notice that your audience wish not to leave after you are done with your presentation, and in fact, they are anxiously waiting it.

Humor is a popular way to liven up a presentation. It makes the audience align with you, and sends a signal that you are in charge. Handled properly, humor enriches a presentation. When considering humor, make sure that whatever content you choose meets four criteria:

- You think the joke or lines are funny
- You can repeat the piece confidently and comfortably
- Your choice is not offensive to anyone due to gender, race, age, disability or politics.
- Your audience will understand and appreciate what you are saying.

If a joke or delivering humor with words is not within your comfort level, consider sharing a lighthearted cartoon such as Dilbert comics, doing a simple magic trick, or doing something else that is unexpected and evokes a reaction and some emotion from the participants.

Here are some tips for collecting and using humor:
- *Jot down jokes as you hear them in everyday life; classify them as your collection grows.*
- *Deliver any humor verbally only and keep things light.*
- *Match your humor to the demographics of the audience.*
- *Research and consider using local humor if you are working off-site.*

> • *Do not be afraid to poke fun at yourself.*
> • *Carefully examine your jokes to avoid being offensive due to gender, race, age, disability or politics.*

Much of the discussion during your presentation will be structured to fit with the learning exercises. If a remark or question is made during a discussion that is off topic or something that should not be dealt with at the time, you can always add it to the parking lot or Q&A session, and return to it during the wrap-up to bring closure. Additionally, if time permits in your presentation, you may choose to hold a general question-and-answer session. Since as the presenter you are in control, you can decide when to stop the discussion. In a large room, be prepared to repeat each question. If no questions arise, be prepared to ask one yourself. You can use an open question to begin the session: "What questions do you have?"

If a question is phrased negatively, restate it. For example, "Why have so many of his staff displayed chronic absenteeism?" can be restated as "Let's explore what we can do to reduce absenteeism in the team." By restating negative questions, you will eliminate negativism and direct audience focus towards the real problem in the question. Do not forget about the parking lot if you receive an off-topic question, you might wish instead to redirect some of these questions to one of the participants. Again, you are in charge, so call upon someone and keep the discussion moving on afterward.

6.8 Present Like Steve Jobs

Yes, everyone can present like Steve Jobs, Apple co-founder and the greatest leader. During his tenure at Apple, Steve Jobs delivered outstanding presentations, new products announcements, and products demonstrations. He sat a new record for extraordinary presentation skills. People around the world admired his very unique and exciting presentation skills. However, by watching Jobs presentations, you can learn the basics and secret ingredients behind such remarkable presentations. With patience, dedication, and perseverance, you will be able to learn the skills and present like Steve Jobs by following the Jobs 8 steps:

1. Set the theme with single headline.
2. Provide the presentation outline.
3. Demonstrate excitement and enthusiasm.
4. Sell an experience, not just numbers or products.
5. Make presentations visual and simple.
6. Treat it like a show.
7. Rehearse, Rehearse and Rehearse.
8. And, One more thing.

Setting the theme with single headline

In all his presentations at Apple, Steve Jobs sets the theme with one single headline. It is the creation of MP3 player, reinventing the phone, or creating a new tablet category. Just one simple statement, one simple theme and one simple focus, that is clear and consistent throughout the presentation. Your audience knows that there are here in your presentation for one simple thing, hence, they will remain focused and excited to learn more. By having a clear, consistent and simple one headline, you have defined the direction of the presentation.

Provide the presentation outline

Your audience needs to know exactly the flow of your presentation, what would be the topics that you will discuss, for how long, whether there are breaks or not…etc. Your outlines must clear, simple and structured in a way to allow smooth transition between sections. You would never have expected Steve Jobs to talk about the iPhone first, then MacBook Air, then again the iPhone. He sticks to his structured outline and deliver it consistently. By following a structured outline, you will be able to open each section of it, and close it smoothly, which will make it easy for your audience to follow your presentation or your story.

Demonstrate excitement and enthusiasm

Your audience joins your presentation for a purpose. They want to learn or know about the 'thing', but not in a boring way. They have given you the presentation, already, to excite them, show them that you worth their time and attention. This is why in almost every presentation by Steve Jobs, he carefully picked his own words and actions on stage, and so he maximizes the excitement. Very often, Steve Jobs attracted the audience attention by repeating words like awesome, extraordinary, incredible, great, wonderful…etc. to refer to Apple products. Similarly, you can use the same technique to excite your audience about your wonderful, remarkable and incredible product or report.

Sell an experience, not just numbers or products

People get bored quickly while seeing numbers and cluttered charts on your presentations, especially, if you cannot make them relevant and meaningful. In Steve Jobs presentations, he used to relate numbers to something more meaningful. Announcing that Apple has sold 12 millions iPads in a year is not really meaningful, but once it is said that this is equivalent to 32,876 iPads a day, this is now more meaningful and people can relate to.

You also have to make your numbers meaningful and relevant. Instead of saying that your team has finished filing and archiving 568,000 documents, instead, you might have said that these 568,000 documents would cover 10 soccer fields. Now, the 568,000 figure means something to your audience as they visualize documents covering 10 soccer fields.

Make presentations visual and simple

By examining Steve Jobs presentations, you would notice that most of his slides has few words while they are rich in media; photos and videos, nonetheless, without cluttering. In your presentation as well, make your slides simple and visual. Use as little numbers and words, and if you can replace these words with a visual; a picture for instance, then, this is better. Pay attention not to crowd your slides with images, or use images with low quality that will not be easily understood or read. Just make it simple and clean.

Treat it like a show

In a TV show, actors are active, passionate and super excited to play their roles. They perform while engaging with their surroundings, other people and other actors and make jokes and fun. This is what Steve Jobs had done and what you can also do. Make a connection with the audience. Ask some other people to come and join you on stage to demo or try a product, make it lively discussion and presentation, and as if, your audience is watching a show which they wish never ends. Add videos and movie clips, show a video clip on how people responds to your product or survey; for instance. Invite guests or external speakers to come and share their experiences, and make your presentation a really wonderful, unforgotten show.

Rehearse, Rehearse and Rehearse

This is the ultimate golden rule for any presentation. Even the best presenters on the world do rehearse. You should never underestimate the power of rehearsing, no matter how confident you think you are, you have to rehearse, and you must rehearse, not even once, but twice and thrice. Rehearsing could give you insights on how you behave, how you talk, how you present, and it allows you to monitor and adjust your body language.

Rehearsing, additionally, would allow you to confirm your understanding of the presentation material, and confirm that there are no dark spots, or jargons. It also allows you to confirm that the presentation content; material, audio, video, images, colors, fonts... etc. are adequate, relevant and appropriate for your presentation and its audience. As an effective presenter, you should never go to a presentation without rehearsing.

And, One more thing

In his presentations, Steve Jobs always left one thing, one final thing unannounced, and always left it to the end of his presentations. These could be a new feature, an extra bonus or just a famous musical band that has joined the presentation to entertain everybody. Give your audience an extra bonus, keep one thing, only one thing to the last part of your presentation, and hint the audience that there will be a great thing towards the end. By doing this, you would get everyone's attention till the end and people would be excited to learn what is that; one more thing.

Presenting like Steve Jobs does not require a miracle, it requires a plan, it requires dedication, and it requires perseverance.

Chapter 6 – Effective Presentation Skills

Q1- In delivering effective presentations, you must first:
- A- Find the right room
- B- Perform needs analysis
- C- Design a compelling material
- D- Get technology ready

Q2- _____ focuses on analyzing problems and focusing on the 20% of causes that generate 80% of problems
- A- Force Field Analysis
- B- Galileo Analysis
- C- Delphi Technique
- D- Pareto Analysis

Q3- During his meeting, Frank needs to evaluate various proposed solutions to the main defect in the computer systems ACME Inc is selling. There were more than 12 solutions proposed by various team members, managers and Sr. VPs. To make sure the evaluation remains transparent and anonymous, you suggest to Frank to use:
- A- Force Field Analysis
- B- Brainstorming
- C- Delphi Technique
- D- Ranking

Q4- _____ uses the Who, What, When, Where, Why and How to generate ideas and data.
- A- Journalist Questions
- B- Brainstorming
- C- Pareto Analysis
- D- Force Field Analysis

Q5- To deliver great PowerPoint presentation, the presenter needs to make sure:
- A- Each slide is full of texts and colorful charts
- B- Allow only 7-8 lines of text per slide
- C- Use various fonts faces and sizes to attract the audience
- D- Use light colors on light background

Q6- The EIEI model stands for:
- A- Engage, Inform, Enable, Inspire
- B- Excite, Inform, Engage, Inspire
- C- Engage, Identify, Enable, Inspire
- D- Excite, Identify, Engage, Inspire

Q7- Sally has been preparing for her presentation for days, and she approached you for one and only one advice that you may offer her to make sure the presentation is delivered effective. The most important advice would be:
- A- Using the right technology
- B- Make presentation simple and visual
- C- Rehearse
- D- Focus on the content

Q8- After one-hour presentation, Juan's audience were happy and super excited about the company new USB device that offers 'Seamless plug & play with your PC'. This is an example:
- A- Simple presentation
- B- Lesson Plan
- C- Setting the theme with single headline
- D- Presentation Outline

Q9- The main objective of performing needs analysis is:
- A- To measure what skills the audience has and what they expect from the presentation
- B- To measure the current presentation needs
- C- To identify main resources required for the presentation
- D- To identify the difficult participants

Q10- Jordan is a funny person, and often uses jokes and humor to liven up his presentations. A key suggestion you would offer Jordan is:
- A- Carefully examine his jokes to avoid offensive due to gender, race, age…etc.
- B- The jokes must be short and direct
- C- Jokes must be offered after the presentation
- D- Not to make fun of himself

Answers

Q1- The correct answer is (B-Perform needs analysis)

Q2- The correct answer is (D-Pareto Analysis)

Q3- The correct answer is (C-Delphi Technique) as it allows for anonymous generating and discussions of ideas and solutions.

Q4- The correct answer is (A-Journalist Questions)

Q5- The correct answer is (B-Allow only 7-8 lines of text per slide)

Q6- The correct answer is (B-Excite, Inform, Engage, Inspire)

Q7- The correct answer is (C-Rehearse) as it is the most important element to make sure the presentation is delivered successfully and effectively. Making the presentation simple and visual is also important, but rehearsal is more important as it will enable the presenter to overcome any pitfalls in the presentation content. Finally, presenters focus on the audience and not the content.

Q8- The correct answer is (C-Setting the theme with single headline). This is what makes Juan presentation exciting and easy to follow.

Q9- The correct answer is (A-To measure what skills the audience has and what they expect from the presentation)

Q10- The correct answer is (A-Carefully examine his jokes to avoid offensive due to gender, race, age…etc.).

Certified Sales Leadership Professional Body Of Knowledge 'CSLPBOK'

EFFECTIVE NEGOTIATION STRATEGIES

- Understanding Negotiation
- Getting Prepared
- Negotiation Framework
- Phase One: Exchanging Information
- Phase Two: Bargaining
- Getting To Yes
- Phase Three: Closing
- Negotiation Challenges
- Negotiating By Phone Or Email

Although people often think of boardrooms, suits, and million dollar deals when they hear the word *negotiation*, the truth is that we negotiate all the time. In workplaces, you negotiate to get more resources to deliver your project, you negotiate to push a due date forward, or seek additional budget. We negotiate almost everything in our workplaces. As a leader or a manager, you have to master negotiation skills, understand the phases of negotiation, tools to use during a negotiation, and ways to build win-win solutions for all those involved.

7.1 Understanding Negotiation

There are two basic types of negotiations, integrative and distributive negotiations. Integrative negotiations are based on cooperation, in which both parties believe they can walk away with something they want without giving up something important. The dominant approach in integrative negotiations is problem solving. Integrative negotiations involve:

- **Multiple issues.** This allows each party to make concessions on less important issues in return for concessions from the other party on more important issues.
- **Information sharing.** This is an essential part of problem solving.
- **Bridge building.** The success of integrative negotiations depends on a spirit of trust and cooperation.

In negotiations, knowledge truly is power.

Distributive negotiations involve a fixed pie. There is only so much to go around and each party wants as big a slice as possible. In this type of negotiation, the parties are less interested in forming a relationship or creating a positive impression. Distributive relationships involve:

- **Keeping information confidential.** Each party hides their actual need to secure a deal from the other party.

- **Trying to extract information from the other party.** In a negotiation, knowledge truly is power. The more you know about the other party's situation, the stronger your bargaining position is.

- **Letting the other party make the first offer.** It might be just what you were planning to offer yourself!

Then, a typical negotiation process goes into three phases; exchanging information, bargaining and closing. These phases describe the negotiation process itself. Before the process begins, both parties need to prepare for the negotiation. This involves establishing their bargaining position by defining their BATNA, WATNA, and WAP. It also involves gathering information about the issues to be addressed in the negotiation. After the negotiation, both parties should work to restore relationships that may have been frayed by the negotiation process.

It is essential to pay attention to all the phases of negotiation. Without the first phase; the exchange of information, and the establishment of bargaining positions, the second phase cannot happen in any meaningful sense because no one knows where they stand. It sets a scene for demands to be manageable and reasonable. Negotiations are, after all, about the art of the possible. Without the third phase, anything that has been decided during phase two cannot be formalized and will not take hold; leading to the necessity for further negotiation or an absolute breakdown in a relationship.

As a negotiator, you are expected to be effective in speaking and listening. You should also demonstrate a positive attitude and respect the other party. Without the these factors, negotiations will be difficult if not impossible. The necessity for negotiation arises because neither party will be able to get everything they want. Knowing that there must be concessions, each party in the negotiation is required to adopt an attitude of understanding that they must get the best deal possible in a way which is acceptable to the other party. The importance of effective speaking and listening is clear; it is necessary to establish what you are looking for and what you are prepared to accept, while understanding what the other parties will be happy with.

A sense of humor and a positive attitude are essential because they allow for a sense of give and take. Negotiations can become fraught, and having the ability to see the other side's point of view while being sanguine with regard to what you can achieve will be essential. Of course you will want as much as you can get, but the other side needs to achieve what they can, too. Seriously uneven negotiations will simply lead to further problems along the line. An atmosphere of respect is essential. If you do not make concessions while demanding them from your counterpart, it makes for a negotiation which will end in dissatisfaction.

However important a sense of understanding for your opponent may be, it is also necessary to have the confidence to not settle for less than you feel is fair. Good negotiators understand the importance of balance. Yes, you will have to make concessions, but the point of making concessions is to secure what you can get, so you need to pay attention to your bottom line and ensure you are not beaten down to a minimum. Knowing what is realistic, and ensuring that you can get the best deal, relies on being ready to insist upon something that the other side may not be willing to give initially. Emotional intelligence, persistence, patience, and creativity can all play a part here.

A typical negotiation process goes into three stages:
1. *Exchanging Information*
2. *Bargaining*
3. *Closing*

7.2 Getting Prepared

Like any challenging task, negotiation requires preparation. Before you begin a negotiation, you need to define what you hope to get out of it, what you will settle for, and what you consider unacceptable. You also need to prepare yourself personally and the key to personal preparation is to approach the negotiation with self-confidence and a positive attitude. Without this preparation, you will end up giving more than you get from negotiations. It may be unavoidable that you will have to give up more than you would ordinarily be willing to, but finding the balance between acceptable concessions and getting the best deal for yourself relies on you being ready to go into negotiations with the strongest bargaining position you can.

In most negotiations, the parties are influenced by their assumptions about what they think are the alternatives to a negotiated agreement. Often the parties have an unrealistic idea of what these alternatives are, and they are unwilling to make concessions because they think they can do just as well without negotiating. If you do not have a clear idea of your **WATNA** (Worst Alternative to a Negotiated Agreement) and **BATNA** (Best Alternative to a Negotiated Agreement), you will negotiate poorly based on false notions about what you can expect without an agreement.

Often the parties in a negotiation need to decide how likely a particular outcome will be. If your WATNA is something that would be difficult for you to accept, but the likelihood of it happening is small, you might not feel compelled to give up much in negotiations. Realism is essential in this situation. If you could have the ideal situation, the "blue sky" scenario, negotiations would not be necessary. In order to focus on the negotiations with a sense of purpose, your WATNA is important. What is often referred to as the "worst case scenario" is something that any sensible person will think about before embarking on any initiative. What if it goes wrong? How will we deal with that? How you feel about the WATNA will dictate how flexible you need to be; and therefore will be in negotiations.

The BATNA is almost more important than the WATNA. If you look at your situation in the absence of a negotiated agreement, and find it almost unthinkable, you will be pressed to enter negotiations in the hope of getting a satisfactory agreement. The word "satisfactory" is important here. Is the WATNA better than satisfactory? Is the BATNA worse? Generally, people only enter into negotiations because they feel they have to. They arrive at this conclusion based on analysis of their WATNA and BATNA.

In any negotiation, it is important that you keep your **WAP** (Walk Away Price) to yourself, especially if it is significantly less than your initial offer. If the other party knows that you will be willing to take a lot less than you are offering, then you will be negotiating from a position of weakness. If the other party knows, or has an idea of your WAP then it stops being your WAP and simply becomes your price. Establishing a WAP in your mind, and ensuring that those negotiators on your side of the bargain, and only they know it, allows you to take your strongest possible bargaining position. The other party will try to argue you down from your proposed price, so you will need to remain firm. If they want to pay less, then you may be prepared to agree on a lower price in return for concessions.

The opposing party will then have to consider what is acceptable to them. Rather than push too hard and lose out on a deal which would be beneficial to themselves, they will have their own areas where they are willing to make concessions. However, if they know that you have set a WAP that would save them money, they will simply hold firm at that price. They have no incentive to make concessions to you. In many ways, negotiation is about keeping as much to yourself as you possibly can until you can no longer maintain that position.

Once you have set your WAP, it is essential to keep to it. A walk away price becomes absolutely meaningless if you are not prepared to walk away should it not be met. You should give the impression to opponents in negotiation that you could walk away at any time. They will, after all, not be prepared to stop once they get a price which is satisfactory to them, they will look to wring a bit more value out of the deal for themselves, testing you to see what you will give up. A warning against setting your WAP unrealistically low is that the other party will not take you seriously if you are a pushover in negotiations and they will seek to test you at every turn.

In negotiation, you must be prepared with:
- *WATNA: Worst Alternative to a Negotiated Agreement.*
- *BATNA: Best Alternative to a Negotiated Agreement.*
- *WAP: Walk Away Price.*
- *ZOPA: Zone Of Possible Agreement.*

In negotiation, both parties should feel good about the outcome. Even though the parties might have hoped for a better deal, both got a better price than their WAP. This negotiation demonstrates the importance of keeping your WAP to yourself if you want to negotiate the best deal. Your range in this situation falls between the price that you would ideally, realistically get and the WAP you have set. In an ideal world you could demand a million dollars and expect to get it. In a realistic world, you need to be realistic in negotiations.

You should arrive at your ideal realistic price by seeing what the accepted market value for what you are offering is. By adjusting for your specific negotiating position, whether you are approaching it from a position of need, etc., you can find your best realistic price. Then think about a price at which it would no longer be worthwhile to strike a deal. Your co-negotiator will have done the same. What he hopes to pay and what you hope to get are just that hopeful. The **ZOPA** (Zone Of Possible Agreement) is the area in which the final price will sit, and within that ZOPA you will ideally end up with a price closer to their WAP than yours. If you hint at where your WAP is, the other party will be less likely to come to an agreement that is substantially better than that.

One way to relieve some of the tension you may be feeling before a negotiation is to remind yourself that there is nothing to be afraid of. As long as you understand your position, there is no danger that you will "lose" the negotiation. During and before negotiation you should always be:

- **Polite**: It never reduces your argument.
- **Firm**: This removes perceptions of weakness.
- **Calm**: This facilitates persuasion and compromise.
- **Professional**: Do not take things personally.

Knowing your position before entering negotiations means that you are sure of your "red lines". Things that you are not prepared to consider that would make your position worse than it is now. Many people get pushed into a deal which is unsatisfactory to them because they have failed to prepare for the negotiation in this way. If you go into negotiations with vague ideas, that vagueness will become a weakness in your negotiating position.

The important thing about your position in negotiations is that you should be the only one who knows what it is. Many people compare negotiation to a game of poker. When playing poker you should always be careful to keep to yourself what kind of hand you have. If your opponent knows your position, they will squeeze you to its very limits, confident that you have no strong impetus to push back. When a negotiator knows that their "opponent" has a weak or compromised position, they will instinctively know that they are negotiating with someone who is working from a position of desperation. They will believe "that is what he is decided he is willing to settle for, because he needs this deal. Does he need it enough to give me a little bit more leverage?" and will negotiate from that standpoint.

7.3 Negotiation Framework

Other aspects of preparation to consider are setting the time and place, establishing common ground, and creating a negotiating framework. Even at this early stage, it is important to have certain principles in place. If you allow them to be compromised, then you will already have put yourself in a position where you can be considered as prey for hostile negotiators. Getting the groundwork in place may seem like a formality, but it is the first stage of negotiations, and therefore as much a part of the arrangements as any other.

Setting the time and place can give you an advantage in a negotiation. People feel most comfortable conducting a negotiation on their home turf. Most people have a particular time of day when they feel most alert and clear-headed. If you are conducting a negotiation at your own site, you have control noises or other distractions. If you are negotiating at the other party's site, ask the other party to remedy any distractions as much as possible before negotiations begin.

In sport, every game takes place at a venue, and in most cases one of the parties involved will be the "home team". In the vast majority of cases, where the parties are evenly matched in terms of talent and preparation, the team that wins will be the home team. They are playing in familiar surroundings, where things such as climate and ambient noise are to their advantage. The away team spends the early part of the game acclimatizing to their unfamiliar surroundings.

> *Setting the time and place, establishing common ground, and creating a negotiating framework are important elements in the negotiation process.*

In political negotiations leading on from a war, or trying to prevent one, there is a tendency to hold the discussions in a neutral venue, where both parties are equally unfamiliar with the surroundings, meaning that neither has the advantage and allowing the negotiations to be even-handed. In business, it is rare to have the opportunity to hold negotiations in a neutral venue, and frequently there will be a "home side".

The time of negotiations is also important. Human beings are always in some part at the mercy of their "biorhythms" which cause the body and the mind to function differently at different times of day. Some people, as you will know, tend to be "morning people" while others are more comfortable the longer the day goes on. If you want to build in an advantage in negotiations, it is worth making sure either that the negotiations are held at your home venue, at your most comfortable time of day, or both. Sometimes there will be debate about the setting for a negotiation and often, this is where the first negotiations and concessions will take place.

Sometimes the parties in a negotiation begin by discussing the issue on which they are farthest apart. It might seem like they are working hard, but they are not working effectively. It is often more effective to begin by discussing what the parties agree on and then move to an issue on which they are close to agreement. Then they can take on progressively tougher issues until they reach the issue on which they are farthest apart. This gradual approach sets a positive tone for the negotiation. It also helps the two parties get into a pattern of thinking about issues in terms of shared interests.

Momentum is an important thing in negotiations. If the meeting is continually stalled by disputes over the smallest of issues, the outcome is likely to be less desirable for both parties as the goodwill which is necessary to drive negotiations forward will be extremely thin on the ground. For this reason, having an agenda which is stacked in favor of positive items at the beginning is a way that will work best for both sides. Concessions will have to happen in the end, but if both sides are in a positive frame of mind it creates a positive dynamic in which to negotiate.

Both sides in a negotiation bring their own frame of reference based on their experience, values, and goals. For a negotiation to proceed, the two sides have to agree to a common framework. They need to agree on what issues are being addressed. Sometimes the way these issues are stated will influence the course of the negotiation. Each side would like to frame the issues in a way that furthers its goals. From this, it is possible to see how involved negotiations can get. Sometimes people will use a phrase to describe preliminary negotiations: "talks about talks" and this is a fairly interesting phrase, as it sheds light on just how much is up for debate in the average negotiation.

Before starting negotiations, it is essential to agree on which issues are up for negotiation and which are non-negotiable. Those issues which are non-negotiable are taken off the negotiating table and the parties endeavor to move forward with what they can negotiate on. It can also be decided what form of words will be used in the program for negotiations, making clear to both sides what matters are off limits and why.

Without establishing a framework, negotiations can be extremely disorganized and lack direction. It helps to remember that trying to get a negotiated settlement between two parties who have their differences calls for a great deal of patience and acceptance on both sides that there will be some "medicine" to take, you do not want to take it, but it is necessary, and therefore it is important to make the pill as sweet as possible. Setting a positive framework for negotiations is all about sweetening the pill.

The Negotiation Process			
1- Exchanging Information	2 - Bargaining		3 - Closing
• Identify your key commitments. • Outline Your Opening Position. • Decide whether this will be high ball or low ball. • Ensure that this position is realistic in light of the facts available to both sides. • Allow for movement within whatever opening position you adopt. • Confirm all agreements reached and positions offered.	• Question for information. • Challenge other side for justifications of their position. • Examine and test their commitment. • Present your key commitments. • Explore key commitments. • Summarize arguments and seek acceptance. • Look for signals of possible movement. • Identify and highlight common ground. • Be prepared to concede. • Begin with those of low priority and seek high priority items.	• Never concede on more than possible by your brief. • Use your concessions wisely. • Do not just give these away expect and receive something in return. • Use conditional argument. • All movement should be realistic and contained within your brief. • It should be always towards the other sides' position and not away from it. • Be prepared for larger movements at first as it can build trust within the negotiation. • Continue with smaller movements.	• Emphasize the benefits to both parties. • Carefully introduce the consequences of not reaching agreement to both parties and losing what has been agreed so far. • Timing is essential. • Take Care when making a final offer. Be sure that it is consistent with your brief. • A Small traded offer is often better. A small move by them in return for an extra movement by you. • Ensure that all agreements are understood and accepted before finalization. • This should be well documented and signed at the close of the negotiations. • These should be then forwarded to both parties post negotiations.

Table 6 – *The Negotiation Process*

7.4 Phase One: Exchanging Information

The first phase in a negotiation involves an exchange of information. Both sides state their positions on the issues being addressed in a non-confrontational way. The tricky part of this phase is deciding what to reveal and what to hold back. The "poker" metaphor for negotiating is a very good one, because it describes exactly the way that negotiating parties will want to "allow" each other to think. The information you share with your negotiating counterpart will allow them to read a certain amount about your position. You cannot negotiate blindly, after all, however, too much information given away can really come back to bite you.

Before you actually get down to work, it is a good idea to engage in a little small talk with the other participants in the negotiation. This will help set a positive tone. You might find that you have some things in common, such as hobbies or favorite teams, with the other participants. If you rush right into the negotiation without some initial pleasantries, the other party may feel that you are being pushy and aggressive. For some people, this is a desirable negotiating style, however, it is advisable to have as many strings as possible to your bow when it comes to negotiations. Being human and easy to relate to is far less likely to persuade the other party that you are someone who needs to be kept in check, and may work to your advantage.

Obviously when it comes to introductions and preliminaries, it is an idea not to get too informal. Apart from anything else, this will feel quite artificial when all parties are fully aware that there are issues to be debated here. Formality also lends itself to details being correct, how many negotiations have foundered at an early stage because one participant forgot the name of a counterpart or made an accidentally offensive remark due to ignorance of a critical detail?

Projecting an image of relaxed friendliness with an element of restraint is your best way to introduce yourself. By no means should you give the impression that you are here to bleed your counterpart dry, this will put them on the defensive and entrench their position, to your disadvantage, but it does help to project self-confidence. If you seem in a hurry to get negotiations completed and an agreement sealed, the impression will be that you want to escape from the whole process with a minimum of losses, which will not make you a formidable negotiating counterpart.

 The tricky part of the first phase of exchanging information is deciding what to reveal and what to hold back.

At the start of a negotiation, you do not want to give a detailed statement about your position on specific issues. That is a subject for bargaining. If the other party tries to rush you into stating your bargaining position prematurely, say something like, "That is an important question. Before we get to that, let us make sure we agree on the issues we are discussing today." It may be helpful to think why the other party would be in a hurry to get you to state your position. If they are fixated on that so early in negotiations, the chances are that they have been worrying about it for some time beforehand, and will want to get negotiations over and done with without having to worry about giving away more than they will need to. In such a case, it does you no harm at all to leave them waiting for this information by concentrating on laying down the framework.

In negotiations, one party's opinion on what should constitute the agenda will differ from the other at least in terms of how the issues should be framed. The same issue can be framed in several different ways, and a simple form of words can be quite contentious. Agreeing on the topics for discussion is something that allows both parties to find common ground, while preparing the way for both parties to recognize that they will not complete negotiations without making some movement on some issues.

Holding back information can be a tricky business. You do not want to appear secretive or deceptive, but at the same time you do not want to give away your bargaining position prematurely. The best way to deal with this situation is to attempt to set the agenda for the negotiation. Say something like, "Let us get a few general issues settled before we get into specifics." At the start of negotiations, both parties will, to some extent, be on the defensive and will want to get an impression of whom they are dealing with before they go any further.

By dealing with matters of agenda first, both parties get an opportunity to "size up" their counterpart and think about what they want to get from the negotiation and what they can get. The major benefit of these early discussions is that the first tentative negotiations can be made without making or breaking the whole process. From here, it is possible to have a more realistic idea about who you are dealing with. This can influence how you carry on with the negotiations.

If you walk into negotiations and after preliminary introductions simply say "OK, so this is what we have come for, and we will walk away if we do not get it", then you might as well not be having a negotiation in the first place. Equally, if you hint early in negotiations that you are prepared to settle for a deal which more or less favors your counterpart, you are simply setting the scene for them to take everything you are prepared to offer and more besides. Your success in negotiations depends on knowing what to say, when to say it and when to be silent.

7.5 Phase Two: Bargaining

Now we have reached the heart of the negotiation process. This phase, bargaining, is what most people mean when they talk about negotiation. In addition to learning about the pressures, targets, and needs that might influence your opponents, you might also want to try to get some idea of their usual negotiating approach.

- Do they typically start out with an unreasonable offer?
- Do they try to rush the negotiation?
- Do they try to frame the issues to their own advantage?

Finding this out can be a process of trial and error, but if you have any contacts in the same business who have negotiated with your opponent you can ask them for a rundown of how the negotiation went. This is something which will be familiar to any sports fan, in that teams and players will "scout" their opponents to exploit any weaknesses and prepare to deal with any strength that might make their opponent formidable.

If an opponent has a reputation for always looking to rush the negotiation, it is possible to use that to your advantage. By remaining firm on your bargaining position you will be able to place pressure on them to get the deal done on your terms. If they want it to be over quickly, they will be less likely to spend time wringing concessions out of you and will have to either spend longer in negotiations than they would ordinarily wish, potentially making them uncomfortable and prone to rash decisions, or make a concession in order to get the arrangement in place quickly.

Finding out and analyzing your opponent's pressure, targets and needs is something that should be done if possible prior to your negotiations with them. If they give information in the preliminary stages of a meeting that may be of use to you, then by all means you can duly note that information and bring it into play later in negotiations at a key point. The more information you can find out in advance, the better for you. It will all be useful in negotiation settings.

Some of these techniques are what you might expect to encounter when dealing with a street vendor, but that does not keep more sophisticated business people from using them. The important thing is to recognize them and be prepared to respond to them if they are used against you in a negotiation. As long as you recognize the technique when it is used, you can actually turn them to your advantage in a pressurized negotiation setting. One thing that many of the techniques have in common is that they tend to be used more in hope than in expectation. The Exaggerated First Offer technique is typically made in the full awareness that that offer will not be met, and the hope that somewhere between the $1000 you will settle for and the $2000 you have asked for, the dealer will make an offer which is as high as you can hope for. Experienced negotiators recognize this technique, and will usually respond with what may be an equally exaggerated counter-offer which undercuts what the car is worth.

The techniques tend not to have a lot to do with realism, essentially trying to create a circumstance whereby a customer feels rushed, belittled, or harried in some way into accepting a situation which is beneficial to the person using the technique. If a customer feels that it is a choice between paying $1,500 today or $3,000 next week, they will usually plump for the former regardless of how true the pitch was in the first place. As well as this, some negotiators will attempt to flatter you by saying "OK, normally I would not go anywhere near this low, but because I like you, here is what I am going to do". If you have a firm line to hold to, keep holding it in the face of these techniques and you will hold the power.

> *Keep these ten negotiation techniques and principles in your mind while negotiating:*
>   1. *Prepare, prepare, prepare.*
>   2. *Pay attention to timing.*
>   3. *Leave behind your ego.*
>   4. *Ramp up your listening skills.*
>   5. *If you do not ask, you do not get.*
>   6. *Anticipate compromise.*
>   7. *Offer and expect commitment.*
>   8. *Don't absorb their problems.*
>   9. *Stick to your principles.*
>   10. *Close with confirmation.*

An impasse is a situation in which no progress is possible, especially because of disagreement; a deadlock. There are a number of ways to break an impasse in negotiations. Here are a few:

- If the impasse involves money, change the terms: a larger deposit, a shorter pay period, etc.
- Change a team member or the team leader.
- Agree on easy issues and save the more difficult issues for later.
- Change the list of options being considered.
- Agree to adjourn for a fixed period of time to try to come up with other options.

The risk with an impasse in negotiations is that it can become a point where any movement from either party will be seen as weakness. The impasse can become the overall focus of the spell of negotiations, where the actual focus should be that which is set out in the initial framework as agreed in the preliminary stages. Sometimes in politics, negotiations take years to reach their fruition, because sticking points are occasionally unavoidable. In business, it tends not to take that long but it is essential that you deal with impasses as they occur.

If you want to get around an impasse, the realization needs to be made that it is happening for a reason and that overcoming it will necessitate changing something about the way you are negotiating. If you can see the sticking point, then by all means make that the focus of your change, but failing that it can be a good idea to place to problem on the back burner and deal with something else something manageable which will enable the momentum to be put back in your negotiations.

> *An impasse is a situation in which no progress is possible, especially because of disagreement; a deadlock.*

7.6 Getting To Yes

In their classic book *Getting to Yes*, Roger Fisher and William Ury argue that most negotiations are not as efficient or as successful as they might be because people tend to argue about positions rather than interests. Once the parties in a negotiation commit themselves to a position, they feel that changing their position represents failure. Instead, Fisher and Ury suggest that the parties in a negotiation focus on their interests. What can we get out of the negotiation that will further our interests? That is the question that should guide a negotiation toward achieving mutual gain.

Bargaining Styles		
Soft Positional Bargaining	**Hard Positional Bargaining**	**Interest Bargaining**
• Participants want to be friends • The goal is agreement	• Participants are adversaries • The goal is victory	• Participants are problem solvers • The goal is an outcome that will satisfy the interests of the participants
• Participants trust each other • Participants are soft on the people and the problem. Participants change positions readily • Participants state their bottom line • Participants make concessions • Participants search for one solution	• Participants distrust each other • Participants are hard on the people and the problem. Participants stick to a position • Participants conceal their bottom line • Participants demand concessions • Participants demand one solution	• Participants treat trust and distrust as irrelevant • Participants are soft on the people, hard on the problem. Participants focus on interests, not positions • Participants do not have a bottom line • Participants invent options for mutual gain • Participants develop multiple options

Table 7 – *Bargaining Style*

The key to making both parties to say yes, and reach the mutual gain is to focus on interests, not positions; this requires that both parties create an atmosphere of respect and trust. Creating a mutual gain solution requires brainstorming to expand the pie by coming up with a range of options. Both parties must be innovative in finding ways that would satisfy both of them. They have also to identify shared values to help create options that will meet the interests of both parties, this might also require identifying issues that can be set aside for future negotiations.

One of the problems that arise in negotiations is that parties can feel that they are being marginalized in terms of what they can do and what they can get. They may feel that being in constant opposition means that the negotiations advance at a snail's pace if at all. In order to put in place a mindset where there is a chance for consensus, the parties can look at what unites them rather than what puts them in opposition to one another. The difficulty in any negotiation arises when there are issues where both parties have a philosophical WAP which is too far from that of the other. There is in this case no ZOPA, and no matter how much negotiation takes place there will be a sticking point. If you can remove the sticking point from the equation at least temporarily, you can get in place a situation where there is space for consensus.

The danger of "ignoring the elephant in the room" is that it will not go away just because it is ignored. It will still be there, and although it is tempting to look at things from a "blue sky" point of view and forget about the clouds forming overhead, you can end up saving up problems for the latter stages of negotiations. What you could look at doing is having someone working away from the negotiating table to find a compromise solution, and bring it back to the table when it looks more palatable to both parties.

The first thing to do in a bargaining process is to identify what you personally want out of the negotiation, for instance, you might say; I want a fair share of all new customers or I want changes to the schedule. You can create two versions of your personal needs statement, your ideal resolution and your realistic resolution, or you could frame your statement into several steps if the negotiation is complicated. Another useful exercise is to break down your statement into wants and needs. This is particularly valuable if your statement is vague. This will give you some bargaining room during the negotiation process, and will help ensure that you get what you need out of the solution.

Next, identify what the person that you are in conflict with wants. Try to frame this positively. Explore all the angles to maximize your possibilities for mutual gain. These framing questions will help you start the process.

- What does my opponent need?
- What does my opponent want?
- What is most important to them?
- What is least important to them?

Now that you have identified the wants and needs of both sides, look for areas of overlap. These will be the starting points for establishing mutual ground. When working through the wants and needs of both parties, be careful not to jump to conclusions. Rather, be on the lookout for the root cause. Often, the problem is not what it seems.

7.7 Phase Three: Closing

The final phase of a negotiation process is the time for reaching consensus and building an agreement. A little hard work in this phase can ensure that the negotiation achieves its desired results. Closing a negotiation can mean two different things: First, it may be a question of how to bring different ideas to a mutually agreed conclusion. A second possibility view of 'closing' is what means negotiating parties can use to acknowledge or formalize the idea that agreement has been reached. Recognizing that parties have reached agreement can be quite simple. One can ask the other(s), "Then, have we reached agreement?" The parties can shake hands, make a public announcement, or sign a document. The real issue is that each has to make it clear to other negotiators that a mutually agreed conclusion has indeed been reached.

People have different ideas about what constitutes consensus. When applied to negotiations, consensus usually involves substantive agreement on key issues. Not everyone needs to be completely satisfied to reach consensus, but everyone needs to feel that the outcome of the negotiation is something they can live with. Building consensus is one of the hardest parts of negotiation, because the negotiating parties will potentially have radically different attitudes to what they feel the results should be.

The final phase of a negotiation process is the time for reaching consensus and building an agreement.

Consensus has different meanings to different people. To some, it is unsatisfactory compromise, with both parties ending on a solution which does not give them everything they want. However, the simple fact is that you cannot please all of the people all of the time. Consensus is about pleasing as many people as far as possible. The best solutions, in reality, are the ones which leave nobody too displeased. In an ideal world you could please everyone equally and completely. But this world is not ideal, and the realities dictate that to please one person you will usually have to displease someone else.

This is why you have concessions: if you push for 100%, it is possible to end up with 0%. It is much better, therefore, to have two parties who each have a significant percentage of what they want. Reaching a consensus may have a bittersweet taste for some parties, but it is better to have 50% of something than 100% of nothing.

Building an agreement takes a special skill, the ability to translate generalities into specifics. Negotiators should realize that at this stage of the process the bargaining is over. They should try to create an agreement based on a fair and accurate interpretation of the consensus the parties have reached. At the same time they want to be careful they do not inadvertently give something up by not paying close enough attention to the written agreement.

Sometimes in negotiations, there can be a tendency to arrive at certain principle agreements and think that the job has been done. There is more to negotiation than offering a concession here and stipulating a limit there. If you make the mistake of thinking that the negotiation process has ironed out all of the problems in a deal, then you will find that there is a nasty shock waiting for you when you come to formalize the agreement.

It may help to think of the negotiation process as a news broadcast. It is great to have headlines that will make people sit up and take notice, but in order for these headlines to actually have any meaning it is necessary to write the stories. While the basic principle agreement reached in the negotiation room will be the headline, and what sticks in people's minds, it needs to be backed up with details. A good negotiations team will have at least one "details guy" who is able to get the small print in place after the negotiators have put the outline in front of them.

Once agreement is reached, it is important to clearly agree and confirm its terms. We are all familiar with what can happen when the terms of an agreement are not clearly spelled out. For an agreement to be successful, all the essential terms must be clearly stated in writing. It is quite one thing to have an agreement in theory but it will be essentially meaningless without the practicalities. The agreement which emerges at the end of negotiations needs to be backed up with the "how" factor. What emerges from the initial negotiation is what you are going to go, and possibly when. The "how" is the most important of all, though, as without the firm details of how you are going to put everything in place you can agree whatever you want and it will not matter.

7.8 Negotiation Challenges

Most people are willing to negotiate in good faith. They do not resort to tricks or intimidation. Every once in a while, though, you might encounter someone who takes a less principled approach. You need to be prepared to deal with people who do not play fair. It is not cynicism to prepare for the possibility that someone will try to bend the rules, especially when those rules are unwritten. It is simply good preparation, and realism. Some people are unscrupulous, but if you know how to handle them it need not be the end of the world.

Using environmental tactics to gain an advantage in a negotiation does not happen that often, but negotiators need to be prepared for it. One rather obvious case is the executive who refuses to come out from behind his desk and forces the other side to sit in visitors' chairs. If this should happen, the best response might be, "I am sorry, but I need some space to spread out my notes. Is there a conference room available?" The host of the negotiations is in a position of power. To deny that this is the case would be wholly naïve and counter-productive. However, the way they use this power will differ between hosts. Sometimes you will come up against a host who turns conditions to their advantage, and if you do not at least say something about it you run the risk of your "opponent" feeling that they can do and say anything and get away with it. Even if you merely make a request for an improvement in the conditions, you will make them aware that you have noticed what they have done.

In a negotiation, emotional intelligence involves recognizing how you and the other party are responding emotionally to the discussion.

It may be that you feel you can deal with any environmental tactics that are thrown at you. If you show an ability to negotiate competently despite the conditions which have been foisted upon you, this may well win you the respect of your opponent. You should not have to do this, though, and it is sensible to put your opponent on notice that you will not be messed around politely, but firmly if necessary.

Any negotiation will be more productive if you are able to focus on problems and not personalities. Unfortunately, the other parties in the negotiation may not take this approach. There are a number of reasons why negotiators sometimes engage in personal attacks:

- They may think that this type of behavior will give them an advantage in the negotiation.
- They may see any disagreement with their position as a threat to their self-image.
- They may feel that they are not being treated fairly or respectfully.

Sometimes you can avert personal attacks by demonstrating from the very start that you respect the other parties and their positions. A respectful opening sets a positive tone for the negotiation. If the other party resists your efforts to establish an atmosphere of mutual respect, you might try saying something like, "Let us get back to the issues." If the other party still engages in personal attacks, it may be time to suspend the negotiation. Personal attacks are never helpful, although there may be some people on the opposite side who feel that by acting or speaking in an abusive manner they can intimidate you.

When someone says something against you; it often says more about them than it does about you. It is wise to take account of the factors which have led to their behavior, it may have come at a particularly emotional point in negotiations, or they may just have been attempting to assert some kind of superiority over you. By maintaining your dignity, you will be held in high regard. It helps no-one if you respond in kind to personal attacks. All that will do is give the person who attacked you the reaction which tells them that they have scored a direct hit. You will do better by simply requesting to get on with negotiations and ignore unhelpful contributions. It may seem like an attempt to back out of a confrontation, but it is no sign of weakness if you refuse to respond to childishness.

Recognizing and controlling emotions is an aspect of "emotional intelligence." In a negotiation, emotional intelligence involves recognizing how you and the other party are responding emotionally to the discussion. If the emotional temperature in the room seems to be heating up, you may decide that it is time to take a break. There is little benefit to allowing a negative atmosphere to build in a boardroom and turn into something which can torpedo negotiations at a delicate stage.

You will recognize when the emotional temperature is rising beyond where it should be, because discussions will become less focused, voices will be raised and the silences will be all the more silent. At this point in negotiations it might be wise to suggest a short break for everyone to go and have a coffee, or take some fresh air. You can then come back to the negotiations with the atmosphere cleared somewhat and try to make some progress without the risk of people losing their temper.

It would be wonderful if the atmosphere of every negotiation was warm and friendly, but that is not the way things work in the real world. By their very nature, negotiations involve a kind of adversarial relationship. For a negotiation to proceed, the two parties do not need to have friendly relations, but they do need to keep personal conflicts and unfair tactics from interfering with the process. It is time to walk away from a negotiation if the other party makes you feel threatened or extremely uncomfortable or the other party uses unfair tactics that make it impossible to have an equitable negotiation.

You may feel like walking away is an admission of defeat, and this may inspire you to try and make things work even when the prospect of that happening is becoming more and more remote. However, there are times when the other party simply crosses a line, and you would be well advised to show them that this is not going to be permitted. Calling an end to the meeting, with an invitation to recommence negotiations at a later date, may be the best thing for everyone.

Some negotiators use tactics which are simply and purely threatening to try and ensure that you bend to their will. The reason that many people do this is because it often works. It will, however, only work if it is allowed to work. If people walked away from negotiations every time someone tried to cheat them or intimidate them, then that kind of tactic would die out. It is good to have principles in this regard, because no one ever got a good deal by making concessions to a threatening negotiator.

7.9 Negotiating By Phone Or Email

Negotiating is not just something that takes place in conference rooms with powerful forces aligned on either side of a table, people have informal negotiations every day with their coworkers, merchants, even family members. Even if you are not in a traditional negotiation position, it can be helpful to use the principles of negotiation, discussed earlier, to bring you a positive outcome in everyday life. As a negotiator, you might need to negotiate over the phone or email; hence, there are few guidelines that you should follow.

The phone can be a convenient vehicle for negotiations, especially when the two parties find it difficult to meet in person. But in many cases an agreement reached over the phone needs to be confirmed through some other method. For example, suppose you have a phone conversation with a coworker in which you both agree to do certain things within the next week. A week goes by and the other person has not done what he agreed to. You call him and he replies, "I did not agree to that." It would have been better to follow up the first phone call with an email message that begins, "I just want to confirm what we agreed to do in our phone conversation."

When you arrive at a positive conclusion from a phone negotiation, it can be tempting to just hold on to your belief that you have got the right result, but even if you have recorded the call an unscrupulous counterpart can try to back out of it if they feel they have plausible deniability. Get everything nailed down by following up, and you will be able to put the deal in the record books. It is common sense to keep everything regulated and avoid any difficulties further down the line. In order to negotiate effectively on the telephone, you need to consider few rules that also apply to face-to-face negotiation:

- Pay attention to particular points.
- Listen Actively. Do not interrupt the other party and do not spend your 'listening time' figuring out how you are going to respond to them when they finally stop talking. The better you listen, the better you can learn, and the more likely you will be able to respond in a way that improves the negotiation's result.
- Do not let the immediacy of a telephone call force you into fast and unwise decisions. There is nothing wrong with requesting more time to think about the terms discussed.

An agreement reached over the phone needs to be confirmed through some other method, such as email.

Email can also be an effective method of negotiation, but is has some inherent limitations. In general, it is appropriate to use email in a negotiation when the topic is clearly defined and does not require extensive discussion. Also, negotiation over email could be effective when the expected response is relatively simple and when there is little possibility of misunderstanding. Nonetheless, email might not be as effective in negotiations when the topic is complex or requires extensive discussions. It also not appropriate when the topic has great personal significance for the parties involved or when the topic is likely to stir up strong emotions.

Email negotiation value is that it keeps a record of every correspondence sent and received, along with dates and times, allowing everything to be official. If you have a relatively simple detail or two to be finalized, email is fine. If you have a situation requiring a full negotiation, email should only be used as a preparation aid and a formal confirmation of things decided in a full, face-to-face negotiation.

Chapter 7 – Effective Negotiation Strategies

Q1- The two types of negotiations are _____ and _____
- A- Win-Win
- B- Win-Lose
- C- Integrative, Distributive
- D- Lose-Lose

Q2- The parties are less interested in forming a relationship or creating a positive impression in this type of negotiation:
- A- Integrative
- B- Distributive
- C- Wining
- D- Losing

Q3- Preparation is the first and key step for negotiation. As a negotiator, you have to be equipped with:
- A- Resources, Strategy
- B- BATNA, WATNA
- C- Agreement, Decisions
- D- Roles, Rules

Q4- If negotiation collapses, it is important that a negotiator is ready with WAP. WAP stands for:
- A- Worst Agreement Plan
- B- Walk Away Price
- C- Walk Agreement Plan
- D- Worst Away Price

Q5- _____ is the area in which the final price will sit.
- A- WATNA
- B- BATNA
- C- WAP
- D- ZOPA

Q6- The three steps of the negotiating process are:

- A- Start, Negotiate, Close
- B- Exchange Information, Bargain, Close
- C- BATNA, WATNA, WAP
- D- Integrative, Distributive, Close

Q7- _____ is a situation in which no progress is possible, especially because of disagreement; a deadlock.

- A- Negotiation
- B- WATNA
- C- Impasse
- D- Agreement

Q8- In _____, participants are problem solvers and the goal is an outcome that will satisfy the interests of the participants.

- A- Soft Positional Bargaining
- B- Interest Bargaining
- C- Distributive
- D- Integrative

Q9- In _____, participants conceal their bottom line and demand concessions.

- A- Hard Positional Bargaining
- B- Interest Bargaining
- C- Distributive
- D- Integrative

Q10- In _____, participants state their bottom line and make concessions.

- A- Hard Positional Bargaining
- B- Interest Bargaining
- C- Soft Positional Bargaining
- D- Integrative

Answers

Q1- The correct answer is (C-Integrative, Distributive)

Q2- The correct answer is (B-Distributive)

Q3- The correct answer is (C-BATNA, WATNA)

Q4- The correct answer is (B-Walk Away Price)

Q5- The correct answer is (D-ZOPA)

Q6- The correct answer is (B-Exchange Information, Bargain, Close)

Q7- The correct answer is (C-Impasse)

Q8- The correct answer is (B-Interest Bargaining)

Q9- The correct answer is (A-Hard Positional Bargaining)

Q10- The correct answer is (C-Soft Positional Bargaining)

BUSINESS ETHICS

- What Is Ethics?
- Implementing Ethics In The Workplace
- Employer/Employee Rights
- Business & Social Responsibilities
- Ethical Decisions
- Whistle Blowing
- Managerial Ethics
- Unethical Behavior
- Ethics In Business

A company ethics will determine its reputation. Good business ethics are essential for the long-term success of an organization. Implementing an ethical program will foster a successful company culture and increase profitability. Developing a business ethics program takes time and effort, but doing so will do more than improve business, it will change lives. A company ethics will have an influence on all levels of business. It will influence all who interact with the company including customers, employees, suppliers, competitors, etc. All of these groups will have an effect on the way a company ethics are developed. It is a two way street, the influence goes both ways, which makes understanding ethics a very important part of doing business today. Ethics is very important, as news can now spread faster and farther than ever before.

Good business ethics are essential for the long-term success of an organization. Implementing an ethical program will foster a successful company culture and increase profitability.

8.1 What Is Ethics?

A human being's personal ethics determine individual standards of right and wrong. Ethics allow people to determine what they should do in a given situation. Each person develops ethical standards, and it is the responsibility of each individual to examine personal morals and behavior. In business, ethics refers to the behavior relating to the moral problems that occur in business organizations. People often automatically assume that businesses are unethical. Business seems to be constantly linked to scandals. Given the media attention to bad ethical decisions, companies that practice good business ethics can distinguish themselves in the minds of their customers and their employees. The company culture helps determine the ethics of the organization. It is crucial that businesses behave ethically in every working relationship.

Companies have ethical obligations towards their employees, shareholders and investors, customers, communities, vendors and other companies. For employees, companies need to treat all of their employees ethically. Begin by providing employees with the rights guaranteed to them by laws. Ethical businesses, however, may go beyond the minimum requirements in the way that they treat their employees. For shareholders and investors, there is a moral obligation to pay back investors and meet the needs of shareholders, particularly low-level shareholders. For customers, every business needs to build ethical customer relationships by providing safe products and honoring warranties. Consumers are growing more aware of which companies treat them fairly, and they will support the ones they trust. For communities; businesses have an ethical obligation to be involved in their local communities. This includes communities where they interact with customers and beyond. And finally for vendors and other companies, businesses have to always deal ethically with vendors and other organizations they work with.

 ### *Operating an ethical business has a number of rewards.*

Operating an ethical business has a number of rewards. The circumstances of each company will determine the results of managing ethics. There are, however, 10 common benefits that all companies have when they manage their business ethics, these are:

1. Ethical companies comply with all legal requirements and are less likely to be fined or sued.
2. Consumers are more likely to support a business with a reputation as an ethical organization.
3. Companies with ethical values improve their communities.
4. Ethical rules save organizations from accidently violating the rights of employees or consumers.
5. Employees personal moral standards will improve at an ethical business.
6. A fair working environment facilitates teamwork and productivity.

7. Many successful financial business practices are reinforced by ethical business practices.

8. Established ethical guidelines will lead a company in times of change and stress.

9. Ethical companies retain employees and save money in turn-over.

10. There is personal satisfaction in doing the right thing.

8.2 Implementing Ethics In The Workplace

Implementing ethics in the workplace is a complex but rewarding task. Every individual has a unique set of ethical standards. Allowing each person to follow his or her moral compass will result in varied results. Companies need to focus on implementing uniform ethical standards and rules throughout their organizations. Employees should never have to question whether or not they are doing the right thing. We discussed the top 10 benefits of managing ethics. Implementing ethics in the workplace will also lead to better profits and long-term growth. Unethical business practices can cause immediate financial gain, but they will cost companies customers and employees over time and on the long run. When unethical practices become public knowledge, it is difficult for a business to recover its reputation. Organizations with reputations for being ethical will also find it easier to earn credit, find investors, and expand into international markets. There are also benefits at the organizational level such as convincing employees that the company truly values ethical decision-making. This builds awareness of ethical issues and creates an ethical guideline for employees to follow.

> *Managing ethics in the workplace requires certain tools. Every organization needs a Code of Ethics, a Code of Conduct, and Policies and Procedures.*

Nonetheless, managing ethics in the workplace requires certain tools. Every organization needs a Code of Ethics, a Code of Conduct, and Policies and Procedures, which will be discussed later. These tools direct the organization as leaders attempt to manage ethics.

However, it is important to consider the following guidelines while implementing and managing ethics:

- **Give it time**: Managing ethics is a process-oriented activity that requires time and constant assessment.
- **Focus on behavior**: Do not give vague requirements; make sure that ethics management has an impact on behavior.
- **Avoid problems**: Create clear codes and policies that will prevent ethical problems.
- **Be open**: Involve different groups in ethics program and make decisions public.
- **Integrate ethics**: Make sure that all management programs have ethical values.
- **Allow for mistakes**: Teach employees how to behave ethically, and do not give up when mistakes happen.

The roles and responsibilities necessary to effectively implement workplace ethics will vary with each organization. A manager should be in place to oversee the ethics program, but he or she will need the support provided by other positions. Smaller organizations may not need to fill all of the roles suggested below; nevertheless, it is important for every organization to determine what is needed before executing an ethics program.

- **CEO**: The CEO of every company needs to support business ethics and lead by example.
- **Ethics committee**: An ethics committee will develop and supervise the program.
- **Ethics management team**: Senior managers implement the program and train employees.
- **Ethics executive**: An ethics executive or officer is trained to resolve ethical problems.
- **Ombudsperson**: This position requires interpreting and integrating values throughout the organization.

8.3 Employer/Employee Rights

An ethical organization is able to balance the rights of employees with the rights of the employer. The personal rights of each party may seem to conflict at times, and the privacy laws vary between states. This is why privacy policies are so important. Instituting clear privacy policies will prevent any confusion between employees and employers. When creating policies, employers need to remember that they are obligated to provide employees with a safe work environment that is free from harassment, and this may require what some people consider an invasion of privacy.

Employee privacy is a tangled legal issue. Companies collect detailed personal information about their employees for background checks and other reasons, and they need to clearly state the purpose of collecting this information and how it will be used in their privacy policy. Personal information must be protected and kept confidential, and the employees need to agree to the background checks. Surveillance, drug testing, and searches are points of contention for many employees, and they need to be addressed in privacy policies. Employees argue that they have the right to personal privacy at work, but there are limits to their privacy as more businesses take drastic measures to prevent theft and harassment.

For Surveillance, organizations routinely monitor the phone and Internet usage of their employees while they are at work. Legally, these steps are protected in many countries because the company phones and Internet are company property. Security cameras are also used to ensure the safety of employees. Experts advise employers to include in their privacy policies, a warning to employees that they will be monitored. There are limits to the use of cameras. For example, cameras are not allowed in locker rooms or bathrooms. Always check the legal ramifications of using surveillance.

For Drug Testing; taking a drug test before beginning a new job is common, and employers also have the right to demand drug tests in the event of an accident or suspicion of drug use. Random drug tests, however, can be contested if they violate employee privacy. The policy on random drug testing needs to be reasonable and clearly spelled out. Companies are responsible for keeping drug test results private. For Searches, privacy policies need to remind employees that their work-space and tools are company property, and that they are not respon-sible for any lost or damaged personal property. This should prevent any invasion of privacy claims if an employer who suspects theft searches a locker. Searches should be conducted carefully and with the instruction of senior management.

Companies are legally bound to provide a safe working environment for all of their employees. Employees can sue their employers for not pro-tecting them from harassment. Local and international laws protect the rights of individuals from discrimination and harassment, regardless of ethnicity, sex, religion, sexual orientation, disability, age, etc. An employ-ee who feels threatened or uncomfortable by any statement, gesture, or action may be experiencing harassment. An anti-harassment policy and training in harassment will help prevent harassment and protect the or-ganization. Any harassment in the workplace needs to be confronted immediately and the rights of the harassed employee protected.

As technology changes, so does the clarity about employer and em-ployee rights. Employers have the right to expect their employees to work productively and represent the company well. On the other hand, employees have the right to personal privacy. Advances in technology provide employers with more ways to monitor employees. Social net-working further complicates this issue. Employees often post things online for their friends to see, but employers may be monitoring these posts well. It is becoming more common for people to lose their jobs because of posts on their social networking sites. A recent survey re-vealed that about half of employees feel that their social networks are not any business of their employers, but 60 percent of executives think that they have the right to monitor their representatives' social network behavior. This use of social networks should be included in privacy poli-cies to protect both employee and employer, but many companies cite personal conduct policies to validate their actions.

8.4 Business & Social Responsibilities

Most successful businesses operate with socially responsible business practices. Being socially responsible requires companies to integrate the needs of their stakeholders into the values and operations of their organizations. Stakeholders typically include investors, customers, employees, the community and the environment. Social responsibility strives to consider all of these needs in their business practices. There are different types of responsibilities related to businesses. Ethical organizations need to cover different areas of responsibility and consider the social ramifications of their actions.

- **Legal responsibility**. Socially responsible companies are obligated to meet legal requirements that govern their industries. Health and safety standards and fair treatment of employees fall under this type of responsibility.
- **Financial responsibility**. Financial responsibility is more than turning a profit. Financial ethics cover everything from fair salaries to fair payments for raw materials and services as well as not price gouging customers.
- **Philanthropic responsibility**. Many organizations are being recognized for their philanthropy. Philanthropy can come from donations, service, education, and environmental programs. Some companies consider the environment its own type of social responsibility.

Ethical organizations need to cover different areas of legal, financial, and philanthropic responsibilities.

Sometimes social and business responsibilities conflict with each other. This is particularly true when social business practices cut into shareholder earnings. This is a struggle for most public corporations. Businesses need to provide their shareholders with earning to convince them to continue to invest their money into the company. Sometimes this means scaling back a social program or waiting to implement one. Lean earnings and a poor economy complicate the balance between social responsibility and company growth. Without shareholders, however, the company will lose the wealth that backs social programs and the community will face further losses.

8.5 Ethical Decisions

We should always attempt to make ethical decisions. It is possible, how-ever, for two ethical people to make different decisions in a situation. In business, it is important that people understand ethical dilemmas and the ethical decision-making process. People typically use five different ethical standards to interpret the world around them. For the best results, put the different approaches together and choose the answers that best fit.

1. **Utilitarian approach**: This approach focuses on the conse-quences of actions. The goal is to do more good than harm in a situation.
2. **Rights approach**: Focusing on the rights of all involved defines this approach. It makes respecting the rights of others a moral obligation.
3. **Fairness approach**: Fairness expects people to be treated equally. A fairly based standard is used to determine actions that are unequal such as pay rate.
4. **Common Good approach**: The conditions that affect all people are considered in the common good approach. Systems and laws are created to ensure the welfare of everyone.
5. **Virtue approach**: This approach uses virtues such as honesty, compassion, love, patience and courage to guide behavior.

> *People typically use five different ethical standards to interpret the world around them. These are Utilitarian, Rights, Fairness, Common Ground and Virtue standards.*

It is important to be ethical on a personal and organizational level. Per-sonal ethics influence decision both inside and outside of work. These are based on personal beliefs and values. Organizational ethics deter-mine workplace decisions. Managers and employees both face organiz-ational ethics, and the company should have ethical standards in place. Organizational ethics flow from the top down. Those in leadership need to promote ethical decisions by their example. Occasionally, personal and professional ethics will collide. In the event of an ethical dilemma, it is important to choose based on what is most important and what will do the most good for the parties involved.

There are many different ethical dilemmas in business that are specific to industries. There are, however, common dilemmas that every organization will face. Some of the examples are:

- Honest accounting practices
- Responsibility for mistakes such as accidents, spills, and faulty product
- Advertising that is honest and not misleading
- Collusion with competitors
- Labor issues
- Bribes and corporate espionage

Law governs many of these dilemmas, but an ethical organization will make the right decision regardless of legal issues. Because these issues are so common, it is important to create ethical standards and train employees to behave accordingly.

Before making any final decisions, determine the ethics of a situation; does the decision affect a group or have legal ramifications? Also, gather information, learn as much as possible about the situation, and get the point of view from all parties involved. Evaluate actions and make different decisions based on the different ethical standards. Test decisions and test whether you would be proud of this decision if it were advertised? And finally, implement the decision, and evaluate the results.

However, there will always be temptation to act unethically. These obstacles are particularly difficult to overcome when other people are encouraging you to behave unethically. They may be in positions of authority or simply intimidating, but you do not have to give into them. You have to try to overcome these obstacles by avoiding attacking unethical people. Sympathize with their situation, but refuse to compromise your standards. Make them responsible. Do not quibble. Directly ask people if they want you to do something illegal or unethical.

This removes their plausible deniability. Try to provide them with logical reasons for your refusal to compromise your integrity and remember to stay firm. Make a decision and stick to it and do not let people wear you down. And take precautions; keep a paper trail of your encounters, and be prepared to defend yourself.

> *Overcome ethical obstacles by avoiding attacking unethical people; and sympathizing with their situation, but refuse to compromise your standards.*

8.6 Whistle Blowing

Whistle blowing is either seen as a public service or a petty act of tattle telling. Whistleblowers create public concern over misconduct. Blowing the whistle is not an easy decision to make. While legally protected by some laws in some countries, whistleblowers take on serious personal risks by informing on their employers. There are circumstances, however, that need to be reported in order to protect the public.

> *Whistleblowers point out serious infractions that break the law; risk public or employee health; fraud; or signs of corruption.*

The term "whistleblower" is British, and it comes from the whistles that the police used to carry to alert the public and other police to a crime. Whistleblowers point out serious infractions that break the law; risk public or employee health; fraud; or signs of corruption. Telling on a co-worker who was late is not whistle blowing. Legal protection has been provided to whistleblowers since the 1960s, and the laws have changed to keep up with the times. While there is legal protection for whistleblowers, they do face retaliation. They may be fired for unrelated reasons, harassed, or intimidated. They may find it difficult to find another job because of their reputations as whistleblowers.

There are two types of whistleblowers: internal whistleblowers and external whistleblowers. Internal whistleblowers go to someone within the organization to report a problem. Many companies have ways of doing this anonymously so that the employee will be protected from retaliation. External whistleblowers go outside the organization with the issue. They go to law enforcement or the media. External whistle blowing is the best method for businesses that are corrupt from the top down. Once the whistle is blown, whistleblowers need to protect their rights and possibly seek legal council to shield themselves from retaliation.

Now the question comes; when you should "Blow the Whistle"! Think carefully before blowing the whistle. Doing so is neither fun nor easy. There are situations, however, when blowing the whistle is the right thing to do. If the rights, health, or safety of others is knowingly compromised and no one will fix the problem, the whistle needs to be blown. It is the ethical thing to do. Blowing the whistle legally requires you to have a "reasonable belief" that the violations occurred with company knowledge. This means that others could assume the same breaches occurred as the whistleblower. It is best to have evidence of the misconduct before moving forward.

8.7 Managerial Ethics

Managers have a responsibility to behave ethically and manage ethically. They set the example for all employees and will determine how effective ethics management can be. Ethical management provides a number of benefits, both to the company culture and financial gain of the organization. Ethical management balances the different responsibilities of modern business organizations; the responsibilities of profit, people, planet and principles. All companies are responsible to make a profit in order to survive and fulfill their other obligations. All companies are also responsible for their people; this includes employees, customers, shareholders, and the community. Sustainability and the preservation of resources is a growing responsibility for businesses and businesses are responsible for the planet we live in. And finally, businesses are responsible defining their principles and ethics that govern them and will help them to act ethically in every area.

 The three traits that people identify with ethical management are integrity, transparency, and utilitarianism.

There are many different characteristics of ethical management. There are three traits that people identify with ethical management. First of all is integrity. Integrity refers to the manager ethical behavior and leading by example. Then is transparency. The company and its managers are transparent and do not hide their actions. And finally is utilitarianism. The organization and manager considers the happiness of the people involved in the organization.

Because ethics and values are extremely personal, it is difficult to ensure that all employees will practice ethical behavior. There are ways to promote ethical behavior, however, by simply instilling a few basic rules such as developing an ethics management program, a code of ethics, a code of conduct and creating policies and procedures that reflect the company ethics. It is not enough to simply create codes, programs, policies, and procedures. All rules must be enforced in order to be effective and curb unethical behavior.

8.8 Unethical Behavior

Employees will act unethically from time to time. It is important to be able to identify unethical behavior and address it. A successful manager should also be able to prevent poor behavior and intervene before the behavior escalates. Stress can take its toll on employees, who will occasionally act out at work. When unethical behavior begins, managers need to identify it as soon as possible. Allowing unethical behavior to continue will have long-term consequences for the company. Some typical unethical behaviors include abusing sick leaves, lying to customers, cutting corners and covering up mistakes. The behavior may seem minor; most people are guilty of at least one these incidents. These minor lapses in ethical judgment, however, can lead to more unethical behavior later.

Preventing unethical behavior is much easier than dealing with the aftermath. We have already addressed ways to prevent unethical behavior such as implementing a code of ethics and ethical policies, and taking swift action. Another tactic that can prevent unethical behavior is improving job satisfaction. Employees often react to situations they feel are unfair. Therefore, unethical behavior needs to be addressed carefully. It is important to discuss the situation face-to-face. If the behavior specifically violates company policy, remind the person about the policy. If the situation is a grey area, you may have to explain why it was not ethical. Approach the situation calmly, and allow people to explain their actions. Do not jump to conclusions, and understand that people sometimes need guidance making ethical decisions. Should unethical behavior continue, take the necessary disciplinary action.

> *If the situation is a grey area, you may have to explain why it was not ethical. Approach the situation calmly, and allow people to explain their actions. Do not jump to conclusions, and understand that people sometimes need guidance making ethical decisions.*

Workplace interventions occur when people are concerned about the welfare of their co-workers. Interventions are usually used to help co-workers with addiction problems such as alcohol or drug abuse. They can also be held when assisting co-workers to deal with unethical behavior specifically committed at work. There are certain steps that need to happen if anyone chooses to hold an intervention.

- **Call an interventionist**: A professional is needed to handle the situation.
- **Create an action plan**: Plan how the intervention should go.
- **Meet**: Have the group meet together beforehand to iron out details.
- **Intervention**: Hold the intervention for an hour or two, and dialogue without judgment.
- **Treatment**: Help the co-worker find treatment if he or she decides it is necessary.

8.9 Ethics In Business

Ethics in business requires diligence and hard work. The entire organization needs to be on the same page in order for people to make ethical decisions. It is important to create codes and principles to guide people. The ethical principles and codes that the company uses, however, should directly reflect the needs of the business.

When building an ethical business it is important that the roles and responsibilities of each member of the company are clearly outlined. An organizational chart will help determine how an ethics program will run. There will need to be a chain of command overseeing the ethics program. The interrelationships of these roles should be established along with the ethical standards that must be embraced at every level. Remember that business ethics begin at the top of the organizational chart.

The needs of the organization should be determined by surveying both customers and the employees. Most companies have a plan to gauge customer satisfaction. The company culture, however, is a clue to the ethics of the business. Anonymous surveys allow people to describe how the company runs and what it needs to increase ethical behavior on every level of the workplace. Companies' needs that must be addressed includes company values, personal responsibility, employee participation, conflicts and trust.

> *Companies' needs that must be addressed includes company values, personal responsibility, employee participation, conflicts and trust.*

An organization's ethical principles should reflect its needs. For example a company that ranks low in personal responsibility probably has a bullying problem and needs to create principles that address the issue. There are a few basic business ethics principles that most companies can benefit from instituting; these are trust, clarity, community, accurate records, and respect. Customers and employees react better to a company they trust and they feel trusts them. Organizations must make sure that all documents, codes, principles are clear and easy to understand and keep all records and accounting up-to-date and above suspicion. Organizations must support community involvement and treat all people with respect, regardless of their position.

A successful ethics program needs safeguards and a clear code of ethics. In order to get the most from a program, it is necessary to evaluate and make adjustments from time to time. Becoming an ethical business is a process that takes time, but it is possible to succeed if all those involved uphold the program and continue working towards a common goal. Ethical safeguards need to be in place to ensure ethical behavior. Safeguards take away the excuse that employees do not know better. Safeguards do more than protect the company; they help bring in work. In fact, many government agencies demand that those they contract with have ethical safeguards in place such as code of conduct, employee training and ethics audits.

 A Code of Ethics is the foundation of an ethics program.

Developing A Code of Ethics

A Code of Ethics is the foundation of an ethics program. The Code of Ethics needs to address certain issues.

- **Laws and regulations**: All legal requirements need to be considered.
- **Company needs**: Consider the needs of the organization when creating a code.
- **Ethical values**: Use the ethics and values of the company. Include two examples for each value.
- **Wording**: Make sure that everyone knows that they have to abide by the Code of Ethics.
- **Update the code each year**, and make sure that everyone has a copy of these guidelines.

Once the code is developed and implemented, it is important to regularly perform internal ethics audit to confirm compliance. An internal ethics audit utilizes several different sources. An auditor or a committee, if there is no auditor; usually goes over the information to determine if any adjustments need to be made. The audit is used to evaluate the design, execution, and effectiveness of the organization's ethical objectives, programs, and activities.

There needs to be complete buy-in for an ethics program to be successful. It is not implemented to keep employees from stealing office supplies. Managers must uphold the ethics program by adhering to it themselves and holding all of their employees to the same standards. Managers are also responsible for ensuring that employees have all of the necessary resources to be successful, and that they are fully trained in any new policies or procedures.

Chapter 8 – Business Ethics

Q1- _____ is essential for the long-term success of an organization
- A- Financial stability
- B- Tested Leadership
- C- Competent Management
- D- Good Business Ethics

Q2- The main elements for an ethical program comprises of:
- A- People, Processes, Tools
- B- Code of Ethics, Code of Conduct, Policies and Procedures
- C- Documents, Processes
- D- Leadership and Management

Q3- _____ is a position that requires interpreting and integrating values throughout the organization. Often, plays the ultimate level of escalation for ethical disputes
- A- CEO
- B- Steering Committee
- C- Ethics Committee
- D- Ombudsperson

Q4- Ethical organizations need to cover different areas of _____, _____, and _____ responsibility.
- A- Legal, financial, philanthropic
- B- Community, corporate, personal
- C- Product, project, service
- D- Corporate, departmental, team

Q5- Steve has been challenged with a conflict of interest in his project. His approach to resolve such unethical issue focuses on the consequences of actions and offer more good than harm. His approach is"
- A- Rights approach
- B- Utilitarian approach
- C- Fairness approach
- D- Virtue approach

Q6- _____ point out serious infractions that break the law; risk public or employee health; fraud; or signs of corruption.
- A- Leaders
- B- Managers
- C- Ethics Committee
- D- Whistleblowers

Q7- _____ refers to the manager ethical behavior and leading by example
- A- Integration
- B- Integrity
- C- Transparency
- D- Actioned Leadership

Q8- The main responsibility for an ethical manager is to:
- A- Report unethical practices to police
- B- Report unethical practices to HR
- C- Identify unethical practices ASAP
- D- Allow unethical practices to continue with short term harm

Q9-_____ is the foundation of an ethics program
- A- Code of Ethics
- B- Steering Committee
- C- Ethics Committee
- D- Management

Q10-_____ defines honesty, compassion, love, patience and courage to guide behavior.
- A- Ethics Committee
- B- Code of Ethics
- C- Virtue Approach
- D- Top Management

Answers

Q1- The correct answer is (D-Good Business Ethics)

Q2- The correct answer is (B-Code of Ethics, Code of Conduct, Policies and Procedures)

Q3- The correct answer is (D-Ombudsperson)

Q4- The correct answer is (A-Legal, financial, philanthropic)

Q5- The correct answer is (B-Utilitarian approach)

Q6- The correct answer is (D- Whistleblowers)

Q7- The correct answer is (B-Integrity)

Q8- The correct answer is (C-Identify unethical practices ASAP)

Q9- The correct answer is (A-Code of Ethics)

Q10- The correct answer is (C-Virtue Approach)

Glossary

Absenteeism – habitual absence from work

Accountability – responsibility to someone or for some activity

Aggressive – having or showing determination and energetic pursuit of your ends

Authoritative – having authority or ascendancy or influence

Bargaining – the negotiation of the terms of a transaction or agreement

BATNA – Best Alternative To Negotiated Agreement

Blinking – closing the eyes intermittently and rapidly Definition not found for

Brevity – the attribute of being brief or fleeting; the use of brief expressions

Clutter – a confused multitude of things

Code – a set of rules or principles or laws, especially written ones

Communication – something that is communicated by or to or between people or groups; the activity of conveying information

Communication Barrier – a structure or object that impedes free communication

Compromise – a middle way between two extremes; an accommodation in which both sides make concessions

Conduct – manner of acting or controlling yourself; (behavioral attributes) the way a person behaves toward other people

Confidential – available only to persons authorized to see documents so classified

Cues – a thing said or done that serves as a signal to an actor or other performer to enter or to begin their speech or performance

Culture – the tastes in art and manners that are favored by a social group

Discipline – training to improve strength or self-control; the act of punishing; the trait of being well behaved

Dismissal – the termination of someone›s employment; official notice that you have been fired from your job

Dyads – something that consists of two elements or parts

Emotional intelligence – the capacity to be aware of, control, and express one's emotions, and to handle interpersonal relationships judiciously and empathetically.

Ethics – the philosophical study of moral values and rules

Fidgeting – make small movements, especially of the hands and feet, through nervousness or impatience.

Hostility – a hostile (very unfriendly) disposition; the feeling of a hostile person; violent action that is hostile and usually unprovoked

Impaired – mentally or physically unfit

Interpersonal – occurring among or involving several people

Judgmental – having or displaying an excessively critical point of view

Non-verbal – not involving or using words or speech.

Oral – using speech rather than writing

Orders – commands to work on an assignment

Outline – a schematic or preliminary plan; a sketchy summary of the main points of an argument or theory

Pace – the relative speed of progress or change

Paraphrasing – express the meaning of (the writer or speaker or something written or spoken) using different words, especially to achieve greater clarity

Paraverbal – refers to the messages that we transmit through the tone, pitch, and pacing of our voices. It is how we say something, not what we say

Perseverance – the act of persisting or persevering; continuing or repeating behavior; persistent determination

Philanthropy – voluntary promotion of human welfare

Pitch – the property of sound that varies with variation in the frequency of vibration

Positioning – position of a body

Posture – characteristic way of bearing one's body;

Prejudices – preconceived opinion that is not based on reason or actual experience

Preliminary – designed to orient or acquaint with a situation before proceeding

Probing – seek to uncover information about someone or something

Proximity – the distance between people

Rehearse – engage in a rehearsal (of)

Resentful – full of or marked by resentment or indignant ill will

self-awareness – awareness of your own individuality

Shrugging – raise (one's shoulders) slightly and momentarily to express doubt, ignorance, or indifference

Slouching – with shoulders drooping

Stance – standing posture; a rationalized mental attitude

Tone – a pitch or change in pitch of the voice that serves to distinguish words in tonal languages

Triads – a group or set of three connected people or things

Unique Selling Position (USP) – This is the message that shows consumers how your product is unique and satisfies customers

Utilitarian – who believes that the value of a thing depends on its utility

Violence – abuse, threats, or assault committed in relationship to work

WAP – Walk Away Price

WATNA – Worst Alternative To Negotiated Agreement

Whistle Blowing – the act of disclosing bad business ethics and practices in one's organization

ZOPA – Zone Of Possible Agreement

Index

Certified Sales Leadership Professional Body Of Knowledge 'CSLPBOK'